modern **GREEK**

by **ANDY HARRIS**

photographs by William Meppem

modern GREEK

170 contemporary recipes from the mediterranean

CHRONICLE BOOKS

SAN FRANCISCO

Library of Congress Cataloging-in-Publication Data available.

ISBN 0-8118-3480-8

Manufactured in China

Published in association with Hodder Headline Australia Pty Limited

Distributed in Canada by Raincoast Books
9050 Shaughnessy Street
Vancouver, BC V6P 6E5

10 9 8 7 6 5 4 3 2 1

Chronicle Books LLC
85 Second Street
San Francisco, California 94105

www.chroniclebooks.com

INTRODUCTION

I have been going to Greece since the age of three, when my parents built a rambling cliff-top house on the island of Skiathos in the Sporades. Every summer, we would pack up the estate car, loading it with jars of Marmite, tins of butter, baked beans and ham—what then seemed to be necessities for our survival—and set off on an adventurous journey across Europe. My earliest memories of island life are of beach tavernas, and of falling asleep at the table while my parents and newfound Greek friends ate endless plates of *mezedes* and drank the night away.

Most of the days I spent underwater, searching under rocks for octopus or a glimpse of the elusive *rofos* (grouper), one of the most prized fish of the Aegean. As I grew older, and bold enough to catch such creatures with my spear gun or fishing lines, I would run triumphantly from the beach, throwing my catch on the kitchen table for my mother to deal with. She would enlist the help of a neighbouring farmer's wife, who would cook *octapodi krassato* (octopus stew), *soupies me spanaki* (cuttlefish and spinach) and *kolios plaki* (baked mackerel), which I would grudgingly eat only because I had caught them with line or spear. Slowly, I was introduced to other seasonal delicacies: *hortopita* (wild greens pie) and *anginares me araka* (artichokes and peas) in spring, *melitzanes papoutsakia* (stuffed eggplants) and *kolokithokorfades* (stuffed zucchini flowers) in summer, and *lago stifado* (hare stew) at the start of the hunting season. All of these were brought by the neighbour's husband, Pandelis, who liked to deplete my father's whisky supplies late into the night.

I first began cooking on my friend Nicos Caracostas's *caique* as we spent long summer months exploring the Aegean. Stormy weather often forced us to stop on uninhabited islands where we would dive for *pinnes* (fan mussels), *stridia* (oysters) and *achinous* (sea urchins). Our favourite meal, *kakavia* (fish soup), was made with a variety of rock-fish such as *skorpios* (rascasse), *drakena* (weever), *caponi* (gurnard), *hiloutsa* and *katsoula* (two kinds of wrasse). Simply scaled and cleaned, they were added to a pot of boiling sea water with potatoes, onions, olive oil and lemon juice. Dipping our stale bread into this heavenly mixture will be an everlasting food memory.

By the late 1980s I was exploring the mainland—researching material for my first book *A Taste of the Aegean*—and discovering a diverse world of food lore and recipes in the remote villages of the Pindos mountains, the wide plains of Thessaly and Thrace and the fertile valleys of the Peloponnese. Centuries of Ottoman and Venetian rule had infiltrated the culinary consciousness. Other influences, such as widespread trading by the Greeks around the Mediterranean or the influx of refugees from Asia Minor and the Black Sea, had also left an indelible stamp on the country's cookery. This rich amalgam has been well documented.

What are not so apparent to today's visitors are the traditions inherited from ancient Greece. A continuity of basic ingredients—especially olive oil, olives, cheese, bread, pulses and vegetables—and a steadfast adherence to the seasons make it the oldest, perhaps purest Mediterranean cuisine. In this essentially maritime nation, the real timeless links are revealed further in the love of smoked, dried, pickled, marinated and salted fish. Although some of the herbs and spices used by the ancient Greeks, such as *silphium* and celery seed, are no longer used or even available, many fish recipes remain close to their ancient roots.

Barbounia (red mullet) are still wrapped in vine leaves and baked; many other types of fish are grilled and served with simple *ladolemono* (olive oil and lemon dressing), fried with caraway seeds in some parts of Epirus or slow-cooked in the oven "a la Spetsiota" style with garlic, wine, parsley and breadcrumbs.

The ancient Greeks did not in general like to eat raw fish, perhaps since the time when the Cynic philosopher Diogenes, who advocated self-sufficiency and a simple life, died from eating raw octopus in 323 BCE. However, fish cookery was taken very seriously; Greek chefs were highly regarded throughout the ancient world, and their skills were not dismissed lightly. Their skill and enthusiasm with seafood is best described in this account by a busy chef:

First I took some shrimps, and fried them all to a turn. I baked the middle slices of a huge dogfish, but the rest I boiled with a mulberry sauce. Then I fetched two very large pieces of greyfish cut near the head, put them in a casserole with some herbs, caraway seed, salt, water and oil. After that I bought a very fine sea bass which I served boiled in an oily pickle with herbs. Some fine red mullet and wrasses I tossed on the coals, and served them with fresh marjoram. I stuffed a squid with chopped meat and roasted the tender tentacles of a cuttlefish with a sauce of some fresh vegetables. I smothered a very fat conger eel in a fresh pickle. I snipped the heads off some gobies and rockfish and fried them in batter. I soaked a bonito in olive oil, wrapped it in fig leaves, sprinkled it with marjoram and hid it like a firebrand in hot ashes. Then I poured some water and cut herbs over some small fry and baked them. What remains to be done? Nothing at all. That is my art, I need no written recipes and no memoranda.

(From *Deipnosphistae* by Athenaeus)

Much has been written about the benefits of the Mediterranean diet. It is alive and well in Greece, particularly where people still use copious amounts of olive oil (which helps to prevent heart disease), eat *horta* (wild greens high in antioxidants), and plenty of pulses and vegetables (which are rich in minerals and vitamins). Sadly, increased wealth and urbanisation has led to major changes. The new generation is often weaned on a much higher consumption of meat, processed foods and drinks, and fast-food staples such as hamburgers and pizza.

My childhood summers were an idyllic odyssey away from English comfort food and an essential step toward embracing all the elements of the Mediterranean diet—from tins of butter to newly pressed olive oil, processed baked beans and ham to slow-cooked pulse and seafood stews, and from the rigid format of the Sunday roast to tables full of *mezedes*. Today, I am happiest when I am cooking and eating Greek food, although I also get excited with every other country's cuisine. Perhaps it is the familiarity or simplicity of flavours in Greek food. I know it is not just nostalgia, because others feel the same. I hope that the recipes in this book will inspire people to cook this under-rated, uncomplicated cuisine. Many are traditional recipes collected over the years, others are more modern interpretations that adapt Greek ingredients and cooking techniques to the contemporary kitchen.

Greek food has always been considered the poor relative of other European cuisines. Fortunately, however, there has been a resurgence of interest in its rich heritage. Greek cooking is celebrated in modern restaurants in Sydney and Melbourne, New York and San Francisco. Its artisanal food products are sold in the finest global delicatessens and its wine-making has undergone a remarkable renaissance. I hope this book also plays a small part in establishing Greek cuisine in its rightful place at the head of the Mediterranean table.

CONTENTS

MEZEDES   9

SALADS + VEGETABLES   39

GRAINS + PULSES + PASTA   57

PIES + BREAD + PASTRIES   69

POULTRY + GAME   81

MEAT   91

FISH + SHELLFISH   109

DESSERTS + DRINKS   129

THE BASICS   151

THE GREEK STORE CUPBOARD   155

BIBLIOGRAPHY   158

ACKNOWLEDGMENTS   158

TABLE OF EQUIVALENTS   158

INDEX   159

MEZEDES

THE SMALL DISHES KNOWN AS *MEZEDES* REVEAL THE VERY SOCIAL NATURE OF GREEK EATING AND DRINKING HABITS. THEY ARE EATEN IN *OUZERIES* AND *MEZEDOPOLION* (THE GREEK EQUIVALENT OF SPANISH TAPAS BARS), SPECIFIC RESTAURANTS THAT SERVE SEASONAL DELICACIES WITH CARAFES OF ICY WINE OR OUZO. SOME OF THE BEST EXAMPLES CAN USUALLY BE FOUND NEAR CITY MARKETS CATERING TO RAVENOUS MARKET TRADERS, OR ON ISLAND QUAYSIDES WHERE *CAIQUES* BRING IN A DAILY SUPPLY OF CHANGING SEAFOOD.

Mezedes have their origins in antiquity. The ancient Greeks loved the simplicity of *opson*, small relishes of raw shellfish, pickled fish, and fried or broiled seafood. Today, a typical modern meal always starts simply with olives, tomatoes, bread and dips before progressing to cooked dishes such as *gavros tiganitos* (fried anchovies), *garides saganaki* (baked prawns, tomatoes and feta), *sikoti marinato* (marinated liver) and *gigantes plaki* (baked lima beans). Depending on the weather or season, exciting delicacies often appear on the menu in Greece. They can include tender vegetables such as wild *sparangia* (asparagus), *kolokithokorfades* (zucchini flowers), *kritamo* (samphire) and *paparouna* (poppy shoots) or seafood such as *achini* (sea urchins), *kolitsani* (sea anemones), *fouskies* (sea squirts) and *stridia* (oysters), all with the unmistakable iodine taste of the sea.

At home, mezedes can also become a dramatic meal. All you need is an ample supply of everyday seasonal ingredients. Serve raw or cooked in small bowls at the table, a slice of salty feta and ripe tomato sprinkled with dried oregano and olive oil, some raw mollusks, broiled meat or kebabs and baked and boiled vegetables. There is little need for anything else as the mezedes tend to become the main meal once the drinking begins.

**FRIED EGGPLANT AND ZUCCHINI
WITH SKORDALIA (PAGE 10)**

FRIED EGGPLANTS AND ZUCCHINI WITH SKORDALIA

Zucchini and eggplant are the most commonly fried vegetables in Greece, especially when they are plentiful in the summer months.

FOR THE BATTER:
1 1/4 cups all-purpose flour
3/4 cup warm water
1 egg, lightly beaten
1 tablespoon olive oil
1 teaspoon salt
Freshly ground black pepper

FOR THE FRIED VEGETABLES:
Olive oil for frying
1 large eggplant, 1 pound in weight, washed, trimmed and sliced
4 large zucchini, 1 pound in weight, washed, trimmed and sliced
Skordalia (see page 152)

TO MAKE THE BATTER: place the flour in a large bowl. Add the water and stir until the mixture is smooth. Beat in the egg, olive oil, salt and pepper and leave the mixture for 30 minutes until ready to use.

TO MAKE THE FRIED VEGETABLES: heat the olive oil in a skillet. Dip the vegetables in the batter and cook in the hot oil for 5 minutes or until golden brown. Using a spatula, transfer the vegetables to paper towels to drain. Set aside in a warm place while you cook the remaining vegetables. Serve with a bowl of skordalia as a dipping sauce. [SERVES 6]

TARAMOSALATA / COD ROE DIP

Until it became too expensive, avgotaracho (sun-dried and smoked grey mullet roe) was used in this dip. Nowadays, smoked cod roe is used as a cheaper alternative. It is available in most good fishmongers and delicatessens. Add a little more olive oil or water, if required, to give this dip the required creamy consistency.

5 ounces smoked cod roe (tarama), skinned
3 slices thick white bread, crusts removed

1 medium-sized yellow onion, peeled and finely grated
Juice of 1 1/2 lemons
Freshly ground black pepper
2/3 cup olive oil

Place the cod roe in a bowl. Cover with water and soak for 10 minutes to remove some of the saltiness. Drain off the water. Soak the bread in water for 10 to 15 minutes, then squeeze out all the excess moisture.

Put the cod roe, bread, onion, lemon juice and pepper into a food processor. Blend until smooth, slowly adding the oil while the blades are running. Cover and refrigerate until ready to use. [SERVES 4–6]

FAVA / YELLOW SPLIT PEA PURÉE WITH ONION AND CAPERS

This popular dish is commonly served garnished with onion, capers, olive oil and lemon juice. Other ingredients, such as roasted tomatoes and stewed greens, can also be added. In the winter, after the addition of a little more cooking liquid, it is also served as a warming soup.

1 pound dried yellow split peas
1 large yellow onion, peeled and halved
3 tablespoons olive oil
1 teaspoon salt

3 tablespoons capers, rinsed and drained
2 tablespoons olive oil
1 lemon, quartered
Salt
Freshly ground black pepper

GARNISH:
1 medium-sized red onion, peeled and thinly sliced

Wash the split peas in a colander under running cold water, picking out any stones. Put in a large saucepan with the onion. Cover with water and bring to a boil, skimming off any foam with a slotted spoon. Add the olive oil and salt, and simmer uncovered for 1 1/2 hours or until the split peas are very soft and have absorbed most of the water. Allow to cool, drain off any excess liquid and then mash to a puréed consistency by hand or blend in a food processor until smooth, seasoning with salt and pepper.

Transfer to a bowl and serve either lukewarm or cold. Sprinkle the red onion slices and capers over the top, drizzle with the olive oil and garnish with lemon wedges to squeeze over the mixture. [SERVES 6]

LIMA BEAN DIP

Large quantities of this easy-to-prepare dip are good for parties.

4 ten-ounce cans lima beans, drained
4 tablespoons olive oil
Salt
Freshly ground black pepper

1 medium-sized red onion, peeled and thinly sliced
10 green olives, pitted and chopped
Finely grated zest of 1 lemon

Put the lima beans and oil in a food processor and blend until smooth. Season purée with salt and pepper to taste. Transfer the mixture to a large bowl and top with the onion, olives and lemon zest. Serve with bread. [SERVES 6]

MELITZANOSALATA / EGGPLANT DIP

Like most of the dips, this benefits from an old-fashioned pounding with a mortar and pestle. Chopped roasted or raw tomatoes, capers or dried herbs can also be added. In northern Greece, walnuts are also used in the mixture.

2	pounds eggplants	2	tablespoons red wine vinegar
3	cloves garlic, peeled	2	tablespoons finely chopped
	Salt		fresh flat-leaf parsley
1	small yellow onion, peeled	5	tablespoons olive oil
	and grated		Freshly ground black pepper

Bake the eggplants in a preheated oven at 350°F for 45 minutes or until soft. Peel and discard the skins and scoop out the flesh. Chop the flesh while still warm, removing some of the seeds if too numerous. Place the garlic cloves and a little salt in a mortar. Crush with the pestle until the garlic is puréed.

Put the eggplants, garlic, onion, vinegar and parsley into a food processor. Blend until smooth, slowly adding the oil while the blades are running. Season to taste with salt and pepper. Cover and refrigerate until ready to use. [SERVES 4–6]

TZATZIKI / CUCUMBER, GARLIC AND YOGURT DIP

Greek-style yogurt is available at speciality Greek or Middle Eastern delicatessens, otherwise substitute plain yogurt. To eliminate the possibility of a strong garlic aftertaste, simply crush the garlic to a paste with a mortar and pestle before adding to the other ingredients. Chopped fresh dill or mint is often added, although I prefer to add finely crumbled dried mint or spearmint. This is a great sauce for broiled chicken or fish. In Greece, it is almost always added to one of the most popular street food snacks, souvlaki or gyros pita wraps.

2	English cucumbers	2	tablespoons red wine
6	cloves garlic, peeled		vinegar
	Salt		Freshly ground black pepper
2	pounds (4 cups) Greek-style	4	tablespoons olive oil
	yogurt		

Grate the cucumbers and place in a colander, weighted down with a plate for 15 minutes, so that some of their liquid drains out. Gather up in some muslin and squeeze any remaining liquid out. Place the garlic cloves and a little salt in a mortar. Crush with the pestle until the garlic is puréed.

Put the cucumber, garlic, yogurt, vinegar and pepper into a food processor. Blend until smooth, slowly adding the oil while the blades are running. Cover and refrigerate until ready to use. [SERVES 4–6]

MAIDANOSALATA / PARSLEY DIP

This dip is excellent spread on toast. It can also be used as a topping for gratins or as a stuffing for fish, such as mackerel, baked in the oven.

6	slices sourdough bread,	1	egg
	crusts removed	2/3	cup olive oil
1 1/2	bunches of fresh flat-leaf	4	tablespoons red
	parsley, stalks left on,		wine vinegar
	chopped		Salt
1	medium-sized yellow onion,		Freshly ground black pepper
	peeled and roughly chopped		

Soak the bread in water for 10 to 15 minutes, then squeeze out all the excess moisture. Put the bread, parsley, onion and egg into a food processor. Blend until smooth, slowly adding the oil and vinegar while the blades are running. Season to taste with salt and pepper. If the mixture seems too dry, add a little more oil and vinegar. Cover and refrigerate until ready to use. [SERVES 4–6]

FETA AND MINT DIP

Fresh herbs are often also combined with feta as in this aromatic dip.

1	pound feta cheese, crumbled	4	tablespoons olive oil
	Small handful fresh mint,		Juice of 2 lemons
	washed and roughly		Freshly ground black pepper
	chopped		

In a food processor, blend the feta, mint, olive oil, lemon juice and pepper until smooth. Cover and refrigerate until required. [SERVES 6–8]

DIPS (CLOCKWISE FROM FRONT):
MAIDANOSALATA / PARSLEY DIP
TZATZIKI / CUCUMBER, GARLIC AND YOGURT DIP
MELITZANOSALATA / EGGPLANT DIP

ZUCCHINI-FLOWER OMELETTE

Seasonal delicacies such as wild asparagus, hop shoots or purslane are some of the other inventive fillings used by Greeks for their omelettes.

4 eggs	6 small zucchini with
Salt	flowers, washed and
Freshly ground black pepper	bottoms trimmed
1 tablespoon olive oil	

Beat the eggs, salt and pepper together in a bowl. Heat the olive oil in a skillet over medium heat. Add the zucchini flowers and sauté for 5 minutes. Stir in the eggs and cook until the eggs have just set. Serve immediately in the pan or transfer to a dish. [SERVES 2]

DOLMADES / STUFFED VINE LEAVES

When served as a meze, vine leaves are usually simply stuffed with rice, tomatoes and herbs. Some recipes also call for pine nuts and raisins in the Ottoman style. As a more substantial main course, minced meat is added to the stuffing and the dolmades are then served with a tangy thick covering of avgolemono sauce.

2 tablespoons olive oil	Salt
2 medium-sized yellow	Freshly ground black pepper
onions, peeled and	40 vine leaves, preferably fresh,
finely chopped	otherwise preserved in brine
1 1/3 cups long-grain white rice	TO SERVE:
2 tablespoons finely chopped	Greek-style yogurt
fresh or dried mint	Tomato sauce (see page 152)

TO PREPARE THE FILLING: heat the oil in a skillet over medium heat and sauté the onions for 5 to 7 minutes, or until softened. Add the rice and mint and sauté for a few more minutes. Season with salt and pepper and stir the mixture well. Allow to cool slightly.

TO PREPARE THE VINE LEAVES: if using fresh leaves, blanch each leaf for a few seconds in a saucepan of boiling water, refresh under cold water and drain on a tea towel. If using pickled leaves, place them in a colander, drain off any excess brine, rinse well under warm water and drain on a tea towel. Lay out each vine leaf on a flat surface and place a heaping teaspoon of rice stuffing (or more if leaves are large) in the center of each leaf. Do not overstuff, otherwise leaves will split as the rice expands when cooking. Fold the sides of the leaf over the stuffing, then roll tightly into a package. Line a large saucepan with extra vine leaves to stop the dolmades from sticking to the bottom.

Place the dolmades in a circle at the bottom of the saucepan, making sure they are tightly packed. Pack in two layers if necessary. Add water to just cover them, and place a weighted plate on top. Simmer for 40 minutes until cooked. Serve either hot or cold with the yogurt and tomato sauce as dipping sauces. [SERVES 6–8]

KOLOKITHOKORFADES
STUFFED ZUCCHINI FLOWERS

In Greece, zucchini flowers are most commonly fried in batter, baked in the oven or stuffed and simmered gently in a saucepan as in this classic Cretan recipe.

3 tablespoons olive oil	3 tablespoons finely chopped
4 green onions, including	fresh mint
green stems, finely chopped	3 tablespoons finely chopped
2 cloves garlic, peeled	fresh dill
and finely chopped	1 teaspoon sugar
2/3 cup long-grain white rice	Salt
5 tomatoes, peeled	Freshly ground black pepper
and chopped	24 zucchini flowers

TO PREPARE THE FILLING: heat the oil in a skillet over medium heat and sauté the onions and garlic for 3 minutes, or until softened. Add the rice, tomatoes, mint, dill and sugar and sauté for a few more minutes. Season with salt and pepper and stir the mixture well. Allow to cool slightly.

TO PREPARE THE ZUCCHINI FLOWERS: stuff each zucchini flower with a heaping teaspoon of the rice stuffing, or more if flowers are large. Do not overstuff, otherwise they will split as the rice expands when cooking. Fold the sides of each zucchini flower over the stuffing as if wrapping a package. Place the stuffed zucchini flowers in a circle at the bottom of the saucepan, making sure they are tightly packed. Pack in two layers if necessary. Add water to just cover them, and place a weighted plate on top. Simmer for 30 to 40 minutes until cooked. Serve either hot or cold. [SERVES 4–6]

DRIED BREAD RUSKS WITH ARTICHOKES AND FETA

- 2 tablespoons olive oil, plus more for drizzling
- 1 tablespoon red wine vinegar
  Salt
  Freshly ground black pepper
- 5 ounces mixed lettuce, such as mizuna, watercress and mâche
- 12 dried bread rusks
- 4 ounces feta cheese, crumbled
- 6 marinated artichokes hearts, halved
- 2 tablespoons capers, rinsed

Whisk the 2 tablespoons oil, vinegar, salt and pepper together. Combine the salad leaves in a bowl and toss with the dressing.

TO SERVE: lay the rusks out on a serving platter and top each with a few salad leaves. Pile the feta, artichokes and capers on top, then drizzle each rusk with a little olive oil and grind some black pepper over the plate.
[SERVES 4–6]

STRAPATSADA / SCRAMBLED EGGS AND TOMATOES

This dish is served throughout Greece in the summer months when ripe tomatoes are plentiful. It is also delicious served cold.

- 2 tablespoons olive oil
- 1 pound tomatoes, peeled and chopped
- 1 teaspoon sugar
- Salt
- Freshly ground black pepper
- 4 eggs, beaten

Heat the olive oil in a skillet over medium heat and add the tomatoes, sugar, salt and pepper. Cook the mixture for about 30 minutes, stirring occasionally, until all the liquid has evaporated and the mixture has reduced to a thick consistency. Add the eggs and stir constantly until set. Serve immediately in the pan or transfer to a dish. [SERVES 2]

DRIED BREAD RUSKS WITH TOMATOES AND CAPERS

Paximadia *(double-baked rusks) are very popular in Greece, a staple in the store cupboard for times when the loaf of bread has run out. They are also added to soups, salads and are used, when pounded, as a topping for oven-baked dishes. Look for them in Greek or Middle Eastern delicatessens and bakeries.*

- 12 dried bread rusks
- 5 tomatoes, peeled, seeded and chopped
- 12 caperberries, rinsed
- 2 tablespoons olive oil
  Salt
  Freshly ground black pepper

Lay the rusks out on a serving platter and top each with tomatoes. Place a few caperberries on top of each rusk, then drizzle with the olive oil and season with salt and pepper. [SERVES 4–6]

LEFT (CLOCKWISE FROM FRONT):
FETA AND MINT DIP (PAGE 12)
KTIPITI / SPICY FETA AND PEPPER DIP
RIGHT: FETA CHEESE
FOLLOWING PAGES: (LEFT) SAGANAKI / FRIED CHEESE
(RIGHT) ROASTED FETA AND RED BELL PEPPER

KTIPITI / SPICY FETA AND PEPPER DIP

This is a typical meze dip found in northern Greece, especially around Florina and Kastoria where long red bell peppers are grown in abundance.

3 tablespoons olive oil	2 red chiles, seeds and
1 red bell pepper, seeds	membranes removed,
and membranes removed,	cut into strips
cut into strips	1 pound feta cheese, crumbled
	3–4 tablespoons yogurt

Heat the oil in a skillet over medium heat and sauté the pepper and chiles for 10 to 15 minutes, or until softened. Allow to cool slightly.

In a food processor, blend the oil, pepper and chile mixture with the feta and yogurt until smooth. Cover and refrigerate until required.

[SERVES 6–8]

ROASTED FETA AND RED BELL PEPPER

Feta is an extremely versatile cheese, particularly good baked with vegetables or added to slow-baked beef and lamb stews. It can also be simply fried with dried herbs.

1 tablespoon olive oil	5 ounces feta cheese, cut into
1 red bell pepper, seeds	2 slices
and membranes removed,	Freshly ground black pepper
cut into strips	

Heat the oil in a skillet over medium heat and sauté the pepper for 10 to 15 minutes, or until softened. Cut two 10-by-10-inch squares of kitchen aluminum foil. Divide the pepper equally between the two squares. Top each square with a feta slice and season with black pepper. Fold each square of foil, twisting to seal the edges, and place on a roasting tray. Bake in a preheated oven at 400°F for 20 minutes. Unwrap the parcels and serve immediately.

[SERVES 2]

SAGANAKI / FRIED CHEESE

Saganaki is a two-handled shallow skillet much used in the Greek kitchen. It is a useful pan that can be used to fry dishes before finishing them off in the oven. When "Saganaki" style dishes appear on menus, it usually means that either prawns or mussels are cooked with tomato sauce and feta cheese.

10 ounces kefalotiri cheese,	2 tablespoons olive oil
cut into $1/4$-inch slices	1 lemon, cut into quarters
All-purpose flour for dredging	

Dredge the cheese slices in the flour. Heat the olive oil in a skillet over medium heat and sauté the cheese slices on both sides until browned.

Squeeze lemon juice over the cheese in the skillet and serve immediately. Alternately, remove to a plate and serve with lemon wedges on the side.

[SERVES 4–6]

OCTAPODI SKORDATO
PICKLED OCTOPUS WITH GARLIC, PARSLEY AND OLIVE OIL

The Greeks love octopus probably more than any other Mediterranean nation. There are countless inventive recipes and cooking techniques incorporating the common cephalopod. Served with icy carafakia of ouzo, it is most popular simply barbecued or boiled as in this recipe. More substantially, it is combined with vegetables, pasta or rice and slowly stewed or baked.

1 large octopus, 6 to 8 pounds or 2 medium-sized octopuses, 3 to 4 pounds each

4 tablespoons red wine vinegar

6 cloves garlic, peeled and thinly sliced

3 tablespoons finely chopped fresh flat-leaf parsley
Salt
Freshly ground black pepper

2 cups olive oil

Clean the octopus by removing its beak, turning its head inside out and discarding the ink sack and other organs. Rinse the octopus well and place in a large, heavy pot with 2 tablespoons of the red wine vinegar. Cook over high heat for about 5 to 10 minutes, stirring occasionally, until the octopus begins to curl and turn a pinkish color. Then lower the heat, cover the pot and let the octopus simmer in the juices that it releases for 1 to 1^1/$_2$ hours or until tender, stirring occasionally.

Add a small amount of water if there is no liquid left in the pot. Allow the octopus to cool and then cut into pieces about 1 inch long. Combine the octopus pieces, garlic, parsley and the remaining vinegar in a bowl. Season to taste with salt and pepper. Cover with the olive oil and refrigerate until ready to serve. [SERVES 6]

ABOVE: OCTAPODI SKORDATO / PICKLED OCTOPUS WITH GARLIC, PARSLEY AND OLIVE OIL
RIGHT: MARINATED ANCHOVY, POTATO AND ONION SALAD

MARINATED ANCHOVY, POTATO AND ONION SALAD

Marinated anchovies are usually served with chopped parsley, garlic, olive oil and vinegar. This salad offers a more substantial starter.

1 pound fresh anchovies, washed, cleaned and filleted

6 tablespoons olive oil

2 medium-sized potatoes, peeled, boiled and cubed

1 tablespoon capers, rinsed

1 medium-sized red onion, peeled and thinly sliced

3 tablespoons red wine vinegar
Salt
Freshly ground black pepper

Place the anchovy fillets in a bowl. Marinate with the olive oil, refrigerating until ready to use or for at least 30 minutes. To serve, place the anchovies, potatoes, capers and red onion on a platter. Pour over any remaining oil from the marinating bowl, drizzle with the vinegar and season with salt and pepper. Serve immediately. [SERVES 4]

KRITAMO / PICKLED SAMPHIRE

Samphire (Crithmum maritimum) grows wild on seashore cliffs and beaches. Its leaves are pickled when still young and tender, before the plant flowers. Its aromatic flower head has an aniseed flavor and is also good for pickling. Samphire takes its Greek name because the seeds resemble barley (krithi).

2 pounds fresh samphire, washed and trimmed	White wine vinegar

Place the samphire in a large saucepan. Cover with water and bring to a boil, skimming off any foam with a slotted spoon. Simmer for 30 to 40 minutes until tender. Drain and allow to cool. Place the cooked samphire in sterilized jars. Cover with the vinegar and store in a cool place until ready to use. [SERVES 6]

VINE LEAVES STUFFED WITH BULGUR WHEAT AND WHITING

Although most Greeks would not dream of stuffing vine leaves with fish, I find these easy dolmades an exciting addition to barbecues.

FOR THE BULGUR WHEAT STUFFING:

1 cup plus 2 tablespoons bulgur wheat	Freshly ground black pepper
1 small bunch mint, finely chopped	4 tablespoons olive oil
1 small bunch finely chopped fresh flat-leaf parsley	Juice of 1 1/2 lemons
2 tomatoes, peeled and finely diced	Zest of 1 lemon, finely chopped
Salt	

FOR THE VINE LEAVES:

	20 vine leaves, fresh or pickled
	10 ounces whiting fillets, cut into strips
	Lemon wedges

TO PREPARE THE BULGUR WHEAT: place the bulgur wheat in a bowl and cover with cold water. Leave for 30 minutes or until it begins to swell and soften. Squeeze out any excess water. Combine the bulgur wheat with the remaining stuffing ingredients. Refrigerate, covered, for about 1 hour to allow the flavors to develop.

TO PREPARE THE VINE LEAVES: if using fresh leaves, blanch each leaf for a few seconds in a saucepan of boiling water, refresh under cold water and drain on a tea towel. If using pickled leaves, place them in a colander, drain off any excess brine, rinse and drain on a tea towel. Lay out each vine leaf on a flat surface and place a piece of whiting and a heaping teaspoon of bulgur wheat in the center. Fold the sides of the leaf over the stuffing, then roll tightly into a package. Broil the stuffed vine leaves on the barbecue, basting with a little olive oil, until tender, about 5 to 7 minutes. Serve with the remaining bulgur wheat salad and a squeeze of lemon. [SERVES 4–6]

VOLVI / PICKLED TASSEL HYACINTH BULBS

The tassel hyacinth (Muscari comosum) was widely eaten in antiquity. These bulbs are popular during Sarokostiani, the 40 fasting days of Lent. Small pickling onions could be substituted but do not have their unique bitter taste. Hyacinth bulbs can often be found pickled in red wine vinegar in Greek delicatessens. I include a recipe for anyone who is in Greece, where they are easy to find.

2 pounds tassel hyacinth bulbs, peeled, trimmed and washed	3 tablespoons red wine vinegar
6 tablespoons olive oil	Salt
	Freshly ground black pepper

Place the hyacinth bulbs in a large saucepan. Cover with water and bring to a boil. Simmer for about 30 minutes or until softened. Drain in a colander and allow to cool. Place in a bowl, add the oil and vinegar and season to taste with salt and pepper. [SERVES 6]

GIGANTES PLAKI / BAKED LIMA BEANS

Lima beans make their way into this popular dish and can also be combined with meat stews.

1 pound dried lima beans, soaked overnight	2 large tomatoes, peeled and finely diced
3 tablespoons olive oil	2 tablespoons finely chopped fresh flat-leaf parsley
1 large yellow onion, peeled and finely chopped	2 bay leaves
2 garlic cloves, peeled and finely chopped	1 tablespoon tomato paste, dissolved in 1 cup warm water
2 carrots, peeled and thinly sliced	Salt
	Freshly ground black pepper

Drain the lima beans and place in a large saucepan. Cover with cold water and bring to a boil, skimming off any froth with a slotted spoon. Simmer for 40 minutes or until most of the water has been absorbed. Drain and allow to cool.

Meanwhile, heat the oil in a large skillet over medium heat and sauté the onion and garlic for 10 minutes until translucent. Add the carrots and tomatoes and simmer for another 10 minutes.

Preheat the oven to 350°F. Drain the cooked beans and place in a large ovenproof dish. Combine all the other ingredients with the beans and bake for 1 to 1 1/2 hours or until the beans are soft and most of the liquid has been absorbed. The beans should be slightly burnt on top. [SERVES 4]

PRASSA ME DOMATES
BRAISED LEEKS AND TOMATOES

Leeks are mostly used in pies or combined with rice. They are also stewed with tomatoes and aromatics often, as in this popular dish.

1 tablespoon olive oil	1 teaspoon dried oregano
12 ounces cleaned and trimmed baby leeks	Salt
	Freshly ground black pepper
2 tomatoes, peeled and chopped	

Heat the oil in a skillet over medium heat and sauté the leeks for 5 minutes, or until softened. Add the tomatoes, oregano, salt and pepper and sauté for 5 more minutes. Add enough water to just cover the mixture, and sauté for another 5 to 7 minutes or until the leeks are tender and the sauce thickens. Taste and adjust seasonings. Serve hot or cold. [SERVES 4]

MARINATED RAW ARTICHOKES

Artichokes are usually cooked in vegetable or meat stews. When wild or baby artichokes are gathered, they are also eaten raw, dressed simply with olive oil and lemon juice.

4 fresh artichoke hearts	Salt
2 tablespoons olive oil	Freshly ground black pepper
Juice of 1 1/2 lemons	

Place the artichoke hearts in a bowl of acidulated water until ready to use. To serve, drain the artichokes, cut into eighths and place in a bowl. Add the olive oil and lemon juice, and season to taste with salt and pepper. Mix well and serve. [SERVES 4]

FRIED BANANA CHILES

Long green chiles are mild and sweet in flavor. They are usually broiled or fried, then marinated with olive oil, dried oregano and slivers of garlic.

1 tablespoon olive oil	1 teaspoon dried oregano
4 long, pale green banana chiles, seeded and cut in strips	Salt
	Freshly ground black pepper

Heat the oil in a skillet over medium heat and sauté the banana chiles for 10 to 15 minutes, or until softened. Sprinkle with the oregano and seasonings during the last 5 minutes of cooking. Serve hot or cold. [SERVES 4]

MARINATED MUSHROOMS

Unlike the French, Spaniards and Italians, the Greeks are fairly wary of mushrooms, except in mountain areas, where locals know how to identify all the wild manitaria *(mushrooms).*

1 tablespoon olive oil	2–3 sprigs fresh thyme
12 ounces button mushrooms, left whole and trimmed	8 black peppercorns
	1 teaspoon coriander seeds
1 tablespoon red wine vinegar	1/2 teaspoon salt
1 tablespoon fresh rosemary	

Heat the oil in a saucepan over medium heat and sauté the mushrooms for 5 minutes. Add all the other ingredients and simmer for another 10 to 12 minutes. Transfer the mixture to a bowl and allow to cool. Refrigerate until ready to use. [SERVES 4]

SPANAKOPITES / SPINACH PIES

One of the most popular street snacks, spinach pies are sold at most bakeries. They are usually cut into square or triangle pieces and are served with a paper napkin for eating on the run.

8 ounces spinach, washed	1 egg, beaten
4 ounces feta cheese, crumbled	Salt
	Freshly ground black pepper
4 green onions, including green stems, finely chopped	4 sheets commercial filo pastry
2 tablespoons finely chopped fresh dill	Olive oil or melted butter

TO MAKE THE FILLING: briefly blanch the spinach in boiling water and drain in a colander. Combine with the feta cheese, green onions, dill, egg, salt and pepper in a bowl and mix well.

TO MAKE THE SPANAKOPITES: preheat the oven to 350°F. Unroll the filo pastry and cover with a damp cloth to prevent drying out. Lay 4 filo sheets out on a flat surface and cut into 3 strips lengthways, each strip about 4 inches wide. Brush a filo strip with a little oil and place a heaping teaspoon of the filling about 1 inch from the end nearest you. Fold the corner of the strip over the filling so that its edge meets the other edge and makes a triangle shape. Continue folding at right angles, making triangle shapes, until it meets the end of the filo strip. Brush with oil and place on a baking sheet. Continue the process with all the other strips. Bake for about 30 minutes or until the pies are golden brown. Serve hot. [SERVES 4–6 / MAKES ABOUT 12 PASTRIES]

LEFT (CLOCKWISE FROM FRONT): MARINATED MUSHROOMS
PRASSA ME DOMATES / BRAISED LEEKS AND TOMATOES
MARINATED RAW ARTICHOKES
SPANAKOPITES / SPINACH PIES
FRIED BANANA CHILES
(CENTER) GIGANTES PLAKI / BAKED LIMA BEANS (PAGE 26)

KEFTEDES (FRITTERS)

KEFTEDES CAN BE MADE WITH ALMOST ANYTHING, EVEN OCTOPUS. MOST FAMILIAR ARE THE SMALL MINCED LAMB, BEEF OR CHICKEN BALLS SIMPLY SERVED WITH A SQUEEZE OF LEMON OR A TOMATO DIPPING SAUCE. GREEKS ALSO LOVE TO USE AN ABUNDANCE OF SEASONALLY AVAILABLE VEGETABLES, SUCH AS SPINACH, LEEKS, WILD GREENS, TOMATOES, EGGPLANTS AND ZUCCHINI, BY MAKING THEM INTO FRITTERS. THE VEGETABLES ARE ALWAYS CHOPPED WITH ONION OR GREEN ONION AND FRESH OR DRIED HERBS, THEN BOUND WITH A LITTLE EGG, BREAD-CRUMBS, FLOUR OR CHEESE, BEFORE BEING LIGHTLY FLOURED AND FRIED.

KOLOKITHOKEFTEDES / ZUCCHINI FRITTERS

- 1 1/2 pounds zucchini, trimmed and grated
- 2 bunches green onions, including green stems, finely chopped
- 6 ounces feta cheese, crumbled
- 1/2 cup grated kefalotiri, parmesan or similar hard cheese
- 2 eggs, beaten
- 4 tablespoons finely chopped fresh dill
- 4 tablespoons finely chopped fresh mint
- 1 2/3 cups all-purpose flour
- Salt
- Freshly ground black pepper
- Olive oil for frying
- 1/2 lemon

Mix the zucchini, green onions, cheeses, eggs and herbs together in a large bowl. Add the flour to the mixture, season to taste with salt and pepper, and stir well. Cover and refrigerate for at least 30 minutes.

Heat about 1/2 inch of olive oil in a heavy-bottomed skillet. Shape the mixture into round, flat fritters, adding a little more flour if the mixture is too wet. Cook several fritters at a time for 5 minutes on each side or until golden brown. Using a spatula, transfer the fritters to paper towels to drain. Set aside in a warm place while you cook the remaining mixture. Serve with a squeeze of lemon. [SERVES 6–8 / MAKES ABOUT 30 FRITTERS]

REVITHOKEFTEDES / CHICKPEA FRITTERS

Revithia (chickpeas) are a staple of the Greek kitchen. The best recipes stew or bake them slowly with vegetables or meat, such as spinach, eggplants, tomatoes and beef.

- 2 3/4 cups chickpeas, soaked overnight
- 1 large yellow onion, peeled
- 1 large potato, peeled and boiled
- 1 2/3 cups all-purpose flour
- 1 egg, beaten
- 2 tablespoons finely chopped fresh flat-leaf parsley
- Salt
- Freshly ground black pepper
- Olive oil for frying
- 1/2 lemon

Drain the chickpeas and place in a large saucepan. Cover with cold water and bring to a boil, skimming off any froth with a slotted spoon. Simmer for 1 1/2 hours or until tender. Drain and allow to cool.

Put the chickpeas, onion, potato, flour, egg and parsley into a food processor. Blend until smooth, then season to taste with salt and pepper. Cover and refrigerate for at least 30 minutes.

Heat about 1/2 inch of olive oil in a heavy-bottomed skillet. Shape the mixture into fritters, adding a little more flour if the mixture is too wet. Cook several fritters at a time for 5 minutes on each side or until golden brown. Using a spatula, transfer the fritters to paper towels to drain. Set aside in a warm place while you cook the remaining mixture. Serve with a squeeze of lemon. [SERVES 6 / MAKES ABOUT 15 FRITTERS]

DOMATOKEFTEDES / TOMATO FRITTERS

- 6 large tomatoes, peeled and finely chopped
- 1 large yellow onion, peeled and finely diced
- 2 tablespoons finely chopped fresh mint
- 1 teaspoon sugar
- 1 2/3 cups all-purpose flour
- Salt
- Freshly ground black pepper
- Olive oil for frying
- 1/2 lemon

Mix the tomatoes, onion, mint and sugar together in a large bowl. Add the flour to the mixture, season to taste with salt and pepper, and stir well. Cover and refrigerate for at least 30 minutes.

Heat about 1/2 inch of olive oil in a heavy-bottomed skillet. Shape the mixture into fritters, adding a little more flour if the mixture is too wet. Cook several fritters at a time for 5 minutes on each side or until golden brown. Using a spatula, transfer the fritters to paper towels to drain. Set aside in a warm place while you cook the remaining mixture. Serve with a squeeze of lemon. [SERVES 6 / MAKES ABOUT 24 FRITTERS]

CLOCKWISE FROM FRONT:
REVITHOKEFTEDES / CHICKPEA FRITTERS
DOMATOKEFTEDES / TOMATO FRITTERS
KOLOKITHOKEFTEDES / ZUCCHINI FRITTERS

HORTOKEFTEDES / WILD GREENS FRITTERS

After an early morning picking wild greens, preferably on some remote mountain top, Greek cooks will use a fresh handful to make these fritters for a quick snack, as the rest of the morning's pickings are boiling away in a pot for later use. Use as few or as many varieties of greens as desired.

1 $2/3$ cups all-purpose flour	2 cloves garlic, peeled and
$1/3$ cup polenta	finely chopped
$1/4$ cup milk	3 tablespoons leaves from
2 egg yolks, beaten	fresh herbs such as parsley,
8 ounces mixed leaves such	mint and chervil
as dandelion, amaranth,	Salt
chicory, sorrel, watercress,	Freshly ground black pepper
mustard, arugula, beet	Olive oil for frying
greens, spinach or wild	Plain yogurt
fennel, trimmed	

Mix the flour, polenta, milk and egg yolks together in a large bowl; cover and set aside to rest for 30 minutes. Cook the wild greens and garlic in boiling salted water for 10 minutes, then drain. Arrest the cooking under cold water and drain well. Add the wild greens, garlic and herbs to the fritter mixture. Season to taste with salt and pepper and stir well.

Heat about $1/2$ inch of olive oil in a heavy-bottomed skillet. Shape the mixture into fritters, adding a little more flour if the mixture is too wet. Cook several fritters at a time for 5 minutes on each side or until golden brown. Using a spatula, transfer the fritters to paper towels to drain. Set aside in a warm place while you cook the remaining mixture. Serve with a bowl of yogurt as a dipping sauce. [SERVES 4–5 / MAKES ABOUT 20 FRITTERS]

KAVOUROKEFTEDES / CRAB FRITTERS

Crab is usually boiled and served with ladolemono (oil and lemon sauce). Sometimes it is also added to rice pilafs or made into these easy fritters.

1 pound crab meat	Salt
3 medium-sized potatoes,	Freshly ground black pepper
peeled, boiled and mashed	Olive oil for frying
1 egg, lightly beaten	All-purpose flour for
2 tablespoons finely chopped	dredging
fresh flat-leaf parsley	$1/2$ lemon

Mix the crab meat, potato, egg, parsley, salt and pepper together in a large bowl. Cover and refrigerate for at least 30 minutes.

Heat the olive oil in a heavy-bottomed skillet. Shape the mixture into fritters and lightly dip into the flour. Cook several fritters at a time for 5 minutes on each side or until golden brown. Using a spatula, transfer the fritters to paper towels to drain. Set aside in a warm place while you cook the remaining mixture. Serve with a squeeze of lemon. [SERVES 4–5 / MAKES ABOUT 15 FRITTERS]

KOTOKEFTEDES / CHICKEN FRITTERS

1 slice white bread,	2 eggs, lightly beaten
crust removed	Salt
2 chicken breasts, poached,	Freshly ground black pepper
bone and skin removed	Olive oil for frying
4 tablespoons finely chopped	All-purpose flour as needed
fresh flat-leaf parsley	$1/2$ lemon

Soak the bread in water for 10 to 15 minutes, then squeeze out all the excess moisture. Roughly chop the chicken breasts and place in a food processor with the bread, parsley and eggs and blend. Alternatively, mix by hand in a bowl. Season to taste with salt and pepper.

Heat about $1/2$ inch of olive oil in a heavy-bottomed skillet. Shape the mixture into fritters, adding a little flour if the mixture is too wet to make the fritter shapes. Cook several fritters at a time for 5 minutes on each side or until golden brown. Using a spatula, transfer the fritters to paper towels to drain. Set aside in a warm place while you cook the remaining mixture. Serve with a squeeze of lemon. [SERVES 4–6 / MAKES ABOUT 15 FRITTERS]

PSAROKEFTEDES / FISH FRITTERS

6 medium-sized potatoes,	1 handful finely chopped fresh
peeled and quartered	flat-leaf parsley
6 grey mullet fillets or	2 eggs, beaten
equivalent firm	All-purpose flour as needed
white-fleshed fish	Olive oil for frying
Salt	$1/2$ lemon
Freshly ground black pepper	

Cook the potatoes in plenty of boiling salted water for 10 minutes. Add the fish fillets and cook for a further 10 minutes or until both the potatoes and fish are cooked. Lift out the fish and allow to cool on a plate. Drain the potatoes in a colander and place in a bowl. Flake the fish with a fork. When the potatoes have cooled, season with salt and pepper and mix in the fish flakes, parsley, eggs and a little flour. Mix until smooth. Cover and refrigerate for at least 30 minutes.

Heat about $1/2$ inch of olive oil in a heavy-bottomed skillet. Shape the mixture into fritters, adding a little more flour if the mixture is too wet to make the fritter shapes. Cook several fritters at a time for 5 minutes on each side or until golden brown. Using a spatula, transfer the fritters to paper towels to drain. Set aside in a warm place while you cook the remaining mixture. Serve with a squeeze of lemon. [SERVES 4–6 / MAKES ABOUT 30 FRITTERS]

OUZO IS A FAVORITE WITH MEZES

SEAFOOD MEZEDES

NOT SURPRISINGLY FOR A COUNTRY COMPRISING SO MANY ISLANDS, THE GREEKS ADORE THEIR SEAFOOD. TAVERNAS AND OUZERIE SPECIALIZING IN ALL SORTS OF SEAFOOD ABOUND. IT IS ALWAYS SIMPLY SERVED — RAW, FRIED, MARINATED, PICKLED, BOILED OR BROILED. ON SOME ISLANDS, SUCH AS ALONISSOS OR KALYMNOS, DELICACIES LIKE SEA ANEMONE FRITTERS, ABALONE OR FOUSKIES (SEA SQUIRTS) ARE ALSO AVAILABLE.

KTENIA / PAN-FRIED SCALLOPS

Ktenia *(scallops) are mostly eaten by savvy islanders, fishermen and divers who manage to catch them. Unfortunately, they are not a common sight at Greek fish markets.*

1 tablespoon olive oil	Freshly ground black pepper
12 scallops in the shell, rinsed	Juice of 1/2 lemon
Salt	

Heat a large cast-iron skillet over high heat for a few minutes. Drizzle with the olive oil and then place the scallops face-down on the pan and sear for 3 to 4 minutes. Turn the scallops over so that the shells are on the heat surface, and allow to cook for a few more minutes. Alternately, broil on a barbecue. Season with salt and pepper and squeeze lemon juice over the top. Serve immediately. [SERVES 4]

MIDIA GEMISTA / STUFFED MUSSELS

In Greece there are many commercial mussel fisheries, so farmed mussels are plentiful. Classic recipes combine them with rice or bake them "Saganaki" style with tomatoes and feta cheese. This recipe uses a typical Ottoman stuffing with rice, pine nuts and currants.

2 tablespoons olive oil	1/4 cup currants
1 small yellow onion, finely chopped	1 medium-sized tomato, peeled and chopped
2/3 cup long-grain white rice	Salt
1 tablespoon finely chopped fresh mint	Freshly ground black pepper
1/2 cup pine nuts	12–15 mussels, washed and beards cleaned

Heat the oil in a skillet over medium heat and sauté the onion for 5 minutes, or until softened. Add the rice and mint and sauté for 5 minutes more. Remove the pan from the heat and add the pine nuts, currants and tomato. Season with salt and pepper.

In a large saucepan, bring 2 cups water to a boil. Add the mussels, cover and simmer for 2 to 3 minutes until the shells open. Remove from the pot with a slotted spoon and set aside. Fill each mussel with 1 1/2 teaspoons stuffing and close the shells. Place carefully back in the saucepan, add enough water to just cover the mussels, and simmer, covered, for 15 to 20 minutes or until the rice is cooked. Serve hot or cold. [SERVES 2]

CLOCKWISE FROM FRONT:
GAVROS TIGANITOS / FRIED ANCHOVIES
KAVOUROKEFTEDES / CRAB FRITTERS (PAGE 32)
PRAWNS, CLAMS
MIDIA GEMISTA / STUFFED MUSSELS
PICKLED BONITO AND SAMPHIRE SALAD
KTENIA / PAN-FRIED SCALLOPS

PICKLED BONITO AND SAMPHIRE SALAD

Meaty palamida (bonito) is served in a variety of ways — smoked, pickled in olive oil, freshly broiled, baked "Plaki" style with tomatoes and onions, or fried and served with pungent skordalia (garlic sauce). Smoked bonito can be found in speciality delicatessens or smoked trout can be substituted.

4 ounces smoked bonito, flaked into chunks	1 small red onion, peeled and thinly sliced
1 ounce pickled samphire	Salt
6 tablespoons olive oil	Freshly ground black pepper

Mix all the ingredients together in a bowl. Cover and marinate for 30 minutes in the refrigerator. Remove the bowl from the refrigerator for a few minutes just before serving. [SERVES 2]

GAVROS TIGANITOS / FRIED ANCHOVIES

Fresh anchovies are usually simply dusted with flour and fried. They can also be salted or marinated in olive oil, or baked with tomatoes or green peppers.

Olive oil for frying	Salt
1 pound fresh anchovies, washed and cleaned	Freshly ground black pepper
All-purpose flour for dredging	1/2 lemon

Heat about 1/2 inch of olive oil in a heavy-bottomed skillet. Lightly dip the anchovies in the flour. Fry for about 5 minutes each side or until golden brown. Using a spatula, transfer the anchovies to paper towels to drain. Set aside in a warm place while you cook any remaining anchovies. Season to taste with salt and pepper. Serve with a squeeze of lemon. [SERVES 4]

KEBABS

SMALL LAMB AND PORK KEBABS
ARE TRADITIONALLY SERVED WITH
A SPRINKLE OF DRIED OREGANO
AND SQUEEZE OF LEMON. BROILED
ON CHARCOAL BRAZIERS AT STREET
MARKETS AND FAIRS, THEY ARE
A DISH UNCHANGED SINCE
ANCIENT TIMES.

BOUREKAKIA / MEAT PASTRIES

Following the classic Ottoman style, these cigar-shaped filo pastries are filled with an aromatic ground-meat mix.

8 sheets commercial filo pastry	1 1/2 cups cooked meat sauce
Olive oil or melted butter	(see page 152)

Preheat the oven to 350ºF. Unroll the filo pastry and cover with a damp cloth to prevent drying out. Fold each filo sheet in half and then in half again. Then fold the edges in slightly. Brush the filo strip with a little oil or melted butter and place 1 to 2 tablespoons of the filling about 1 inch from the end nearest you. Fold the filo over the filling and continue folding into a cigar shape until it meets the end of the sheet. Brush with oil and place on a baking sheet. Continue the process with all the other sheets of filo. Bake for about 30 minutes or until the pies are golden brown. Serve hot. [SERVES 4]

SIKOTI MARINATO / MARINATED LIVER

Liver is commonly fried or broiled simply. This recipe adds some aromatic flavorings to make an interesting meze.

11 ounces calf's liver, cleaned, trimmed and sliced	Sprigs fresh thyme
MARINADE:	2 tablespoons olive oil
1/2 teaspoon celery seed	Salt
1 bay leaf, crumbled	Freshly ground black pepper

Mix the liver with the marinade ingredients in a bowl and refrigerate until ready to use. Heat a large skillet and fry the liver with all the marinade ingredients for about 10 minutes over medium heat. Transfer to a bowl and serve hot. [SERVES 4]

CLOCKWISE FROM FRONT:
SIKOTI MARINATO / MARINATED LIVER
KEFTEDES / LAMB MEATBALLS
BOUREKAKIA / MEAT PASTRIES
PORK AND CORIANDER KEBABS
LAMB KEBABS

LAMB KEBABS

10 ounces leg of lamb (boned), trimmed and cubed	Salt
1 tablespoon chile flakes	Freshly ground black pepper
	Olive oil for basting

Soak wooden skewers in cold water until ready to use. Thread the lamb cubes onto the skewers. Sear the kebabs on a hot barbecue or under the broiler. Sprinkle with the chile flakes and season with salt and pepper. Baste with a little olive oil and cook, turning frequently, for about 10 to 15 minutes. Serve hot. [SERVES 4]

PORK AND CORIANDER KEBABS

1 1/2 pounds boneless lean pork, trimmed and cubed	2 garlic cloves, peeled and finely chopped
MARINADE:	1 tablespoon finely chopped
2 tablespoons coriander seeds, crushed	fresh flat-leaf parsley
	Salt
2 tablespoons olive oil	Freshly ground black pepper

Mix the pork with the marinade ingredients in a bowl and refrigerate until ready to use. Soak wooden skewers in cold water until ready to use. Thread the pork cubes onto the skewers. Sear the kebabs on a hot barbecue or broil. Season with salt and pepper, baste with the marinade ingredients and cook, turning frequently, for about 10 to 15 minutes. Serve hot. [SERVES 6]

KEFTEDES / LAMB MEATBALLS

Small keftedes (meatballs) are always fried and served with a squeeze of lemon. As a main course, larger meatballs are broiled or barbecued.

2 slices white bread, crusts removed	2 tablespoons coriander seeds, finely crushed
3 pounds ground lamb	4 tablespoons ouzo
2 small yellow onions, peeled and finely diced	1 teaspoon salt
4 eggs, lightly beaten	Freshly ground black pepper
4 tablespoons finely chopped fresh flat-leaf parsley	All-purpose flour for dredging
	Olive oil for frying
	1/2 lemon

Soak the bread in water for 10 to 15 minutes, then squeeze out all the excess moisture and crumble. Mix with lamb, onions, eggs, herbs, ouzo and seasonings or place in a food processor and coarsely blend. Cover and refrigerate until ready to use. Roll the mixture into small balls and dredge lightly with flour. Heat some olive oil in a large skillet and fry the meatballs for about 10 minutes over medium heat, turning frequently. Drain on paper towels and serve with a squeeze of lemon. [SERVES 6]

SALADS + VEGETABLES

VEGETABLES ARE AT THE HEART OF THE GREEK DIET. TOGETHER WITH OLIVE OIL, PULSES AND GRAINS, THEY CONSTITUTE THE BACKBONE OF THE MUCH-DISCUSSED MEDITERRANEAN DIET THAT, IN ITS PUREST FORM, IS STILL VERY MUCH A MEATLESS ONE. IT SURVIVES IN ISOLATED PARTS OF THE COUNTRY, PARTICULARLY IN MOUNTAINOUS REGIONS AND THE ISLANDS.

In every city and town, *laiki agora* (street markets) are a regular weekly occurrence. Farmers travel in from their allotments to set up stalls selling all the indispensable produce at the heart of the Greek repertoire – potatoes, onions, tomatoes, carrots, green beans and fresh herbs such as parsley, dill and mint. Old women scour fields and hedgerows for seasonal delicacies to sell, such as *lapatha* (sorrel), *roka* (arugula), *koutsounada* (poppy), *tsouknida* (nettles), *glistrida* (purslane) and *papoules* (pea shoots), which make their way into pies and salads.

There are also stalls devoted just to wild or cultivated *horta* (greens). *Vlita* (amaranth), *radikia* (chicory), *andidia* (frisée) and *vrouves* (mustard), boiled and served with olive oil and a squeeze of lemon, are regularly served as popular Greek salads. There are three other classic salads: grated cabbage and carrot salad in winter; finely chopped romaine lettuce, green onions and dill in spring; and the ubiquitous *horiatiki* summer salad of tomato, cucumber, bell pepper, onion and feta cheese.

In rural areas, families still grow seasonal vegetables in gardens and fields for specific home use: cabbages and pumpkins in autumn; celery root, turnips and kohlrabi in winter; artichokes and lettuces in spring; and tomatoes, zucchini, beans, eggplant and peppers in the summer months. All are used in stuffed or baked recipes with *avgolemono* sauce or in *ladera* dishes, delicious slow-cooked vegetable stews that combine olive oil, herbs and vegetables. Vegetables are also frequently boiled, fried and pickled. In Crete and the Cyclades, seasonal vegetables are often added inventively to fish and meat stews.

DOMATES GEMISTES / TOMATOES STUFFED
THREE DIFFERENT WAYS (PAGE 40)

DOMATES GEMISTES
TOMATOES STUFFED THREE DIFFERENT WAYS

In the summertime, large tomatoes and peppers are most commonly stuffed with rice or meat, placed in tapsia *(large metal baking pans), surrounded by some potatoes and baked in the oven. They are delicious hot or cold.*

12 medium-sized tomatoes	1 cup meat sauce
2 teaspoons sugar	(see page 152)
FOR THE RICE STUFFING:	**FOR THE BULGUR WHEAT STUFFING:**
1 tablespoon olive oil	3/4 cup bulgur wheat
1 medium-sized yellow onion,	2 green onions, including
peeled and finely chopped	green stems, finely chopped
1/2 cup long-grain white rice	1 tablespoon finely chopped
1 teaspoon dried mint	fresh mint
Salt	1 tablespoon finely chopped
Freshly ground black pepper	fresh flat-leaf parsley
FOR THE MEAT STUFFING:	1 tablespoon olive oil
1 tablespoon olive oil	Salt
1/4 cup long-grain white rice	Freshly ground black pepper

TO PREPARE THE TOMATOES: slice the tops off the tomatoes and reserve them. Scoop out most of the tomato pulp with a teaspoon to allow room for the stuffing, being careful not to break the skin. Reserve the tomato pulp in a bowl. Sprinkle the insides of the tomatoes with the sugar and set aside until ready to use.

TO MAKE THE RICE STUFFING: heat the olive oil in a saucepan and sauté the onion for 5 minutes or until softened. Add the rice and mint and sauté for 2 more minutes. Add half the tomato pulp and sauté for 2 more minutes. Take off the heat, season to taste with salt and pepper, and set aside.

TO MAKE THE MEAT STUFFING: heat the olive oil in a saucepan and sauté the rice for 2 minutes or until softened. Add the meat sauce and mix well. Take off the heat and set aside.

TO MAKE THE BULGUR WHEAT STUFFING: place the bulgur wheat in a bowl and cover with cold water. Leave for 30 minutes or until it begins to swell and soften. Drain and squeeze out any excess water. Combine the bulgur wheat with the remaining tomato pulp, green onions, mint, parsley and oil. Season with salt and pepper and set aside.

TO COOK THE STUFFED TOMATOES: preheat the oven to 350°F. Rinse the tomatoes under water and dry on paper towels. Fill 4 tomatoes with the rice stuffing, 4 with the meat stuffing and the remaining 4 with the bulgur wheat stuffing, being careful not to overstuff the tomatoes. Place all 12 on a lightly oiled baking pan. Replace the reserved tops back on the tomatoes, pour a little water around them and bake for 40 minutes. Serve hot or cold. [SERVES 6]

PURSLANE, SMOKED TROUT, POTATO
AND QUAIL EGG SALAD

Glistrida *(purslane) is often collected wild and added to salads or omelettes.*

Olive oil for frying and	7 ounces smoked trout,
dressing salad	flaked into chunks
8 ounces potatoes, peeled,	12 quail eggs, hard-boiled,
boiled and quartered	peeled and halved lengthwise
1 teaspoon dried oregano	Juice of 1 lemon
4 ounces purslane, washed	Salt
and trimmed	Freshly ground black pepper

Heat 1/2 inch of olive oil in a skillet over medium heat. Toss potatoes in the oregano and sauté in the hot oil for 5 minutes or until golden brown. Drain on paper towels.

To serve, place the purslane, potatoes, trout and quail eggs on a large platter. Drizzle with a little olive oil and the lemon juice. Sprinkle with salt and grind some pepper over the salad. [SERVES 4–6]

HORIATIKI SALAD

Who would have thought that this country-style salad would become one of the best loved Greek dishes? Tourists eat it every day in the summer months, blissfully unaware of the rich repertoire of vegetarian recipes also being eaten in Greek homes.

4 ounces feta	1 small red onion, peeled
1 red or green bell pepper	and thinly sliced
1 English cucumber	1 teaspoon dried oregano
5 tomatoes	Salt
Handful black olives	Freshly ground black pepper
1 head romaine lettuce, dark	Olive oil for dressing salad
green outer leaves removed	Red wine vinegar

Assemble cheese and vegetables in a large bowl. Sprinkle with the oregano, salt and pepper. Drizzle with oil and vinegar and serve. [SERVES 4]

RIGHT: PURSLANE, SMOKED TROUT, POTATO
AND QUAIL EGG SALAD
FOLLOWING PAGES: (LEFT) HORIATIKI SALAD
(RIGHT) BOILED ZUCCHINI, FETA AND MINT SALAD (PAGE 44)

GOLDEN BEET, SHALLOT, DANDELION AND CHICKEN LIVER SALAD

Substitute red beets and any other kind of slightly bitter leaves if necessary.

2 tablespoons olive oil plus extra for drizzling

8 ounces shallots, peeled and left whole

1 teaspoon coriander seeds
Salt
Freshly ground black pepper

2 tablespoons white wine vinegar plus extra for dressing

1 pound chicken livers, trimmed and membranes removed, halved

3 ounces dandelion leaves, washed

1 pound golden beets, boiled, skins peeled and quartered

2 tablespoons sesame seeds, toasted

TO PREPARE THE SHALLOTS: heat 1 tablespoon of the olive oil in a skillet over medium heat. Add the shallots and coriander seeds, season with salt and pepper, and sauté for 5 minutes. Add 1 tablespoon of the vinegar at the last minute and stir well to coat the shallots. Transfer to a small saucepan, add water to just cover the shallots and bring to a boil. Then, simmer for 10 to 15 minutes until the liquid has almost evaporated.

TO PREPARE THE CHICKEN LIVERS: heat the remaining 1 tablespoon olive oil in a skillet over medium heat. Add the chicken livers, season with salt and pepper, and sauté for 5 to 7 minutes until cooked. Add the remaining 1 tablespoon vinegar at the last minute and stir well to coat the chicken livers.

TO SERVE: place the dandelion leaves, shallots, beets and chicken livers in individual serving bowls or into a large salad bowl. Sprinkle with the sesame seeds, season with salt and pepper, and drizzle with a little extra olive oil and vinegar. [SERVES 4–6]

VLITA / BOILED AMARANTH SALAD

Originating in the Andes, amaranth has spread throughout the Far East. In Greece, a favorite start to a meal is a plate of the vegetable boiled and liberally drizzled with olive oil and a squeeze of lemon. Amaranth is still picked wild, although today most of it is farmed. In North America amaranth can be found in many Asian markets. Fresh spinach can be substituted—use two bunches instead of one.

1 large bunch amaranth

3 tablespoons olive oil

1 lemon, halved

Salt
Freshly ground black pepper

Boil amaranth for 15 to 20 minutes. Strain, then refresh with ice if not using immediately. To serve, dress with the olive oil, squeeze lemon halves over the mixture, season with salt and pepper, and mix. [SERVES 2–4]

ABOVE: GOLDEN BEET, SHALLOT, DANDELION AND
CHICKEN LIVER SALAD
RIGHT: VLITA / BOILED AMARANTH SALAD

BOILED ZUCCHINI, FETA AND MINT SALAD

In tavernas, zucchini and cauliflower are always boiled until soft and served hot or cold as a starter, drizzled with olive oil, lemon juice or vinegar.

2 pounds baby zucchini, washed

4 ounces feta, crumbled

1 1/2 tablespoons finely chopped fresh mint

Salt
Freshly ground black pepper
Olive oil
Red wine vinegar

Cook the zucchini in plenty of boiling salted water for 10 to 20 minutes or until tender. The zucchini should be soft in texture. Drain and transfer to a serving dish. Sprinkle with the crumbled feta and mint, and season with salt and pepper. Drizzle with some olive oil and red wine vinegar and serve hot or cold. [SERVES 4]

VEGETABLES À LA GRECQUE

Although the Greeks do not really ever cook this way, the French à la Grecque method of cooking young spring or autumn vegetables does have a some-what Hellenic flavor, with its liberal use of vinegar, fresh herbs and coriander seeds.

1 3/4 cup white wine	1 tablespoon coriander seeds
1 cup white wine vinegar	1 teaspoon salt
1/2 cup water	6 baby turnips, trimmed
3 tablespoons olive oil	with a little stem left on
6 bay leaves	and halved
1 small handful fresh flat-leaf	3 baby cauliflowers, quartered
parsley, including stems	12 shallots or baby onions,
4–5 sprigs fresh thyme	peeled whole
1 tablespoon black peppercorns	10 asparagus spears, trimmed

Put the wine, vinegar, water, olive oil, bay leaves, parsley, thyme, pepper-corns, coriander seeds and salt into a large saucepan and bring to a boil. Continue to boil over a high heat until the liquid emulsifies. Drop all the vegetables into the boiling emulsion, adding the asparagus last, and cook for about 10 minutes or until just tender. Drain all the vegetables and reserve some of the emulsified liquid. Combine all the vegetables on a platter and pour the reserved liquid over. Serve hot or cold. [SERVES 6]

POTATO, ONION AND CAPER SALAD

In the Cycladic islands, capers grow wild on the cliffs. Picked and pickled by most families, they are added to this frugal salad found often in the summer months at the lunchtime table.

2 1/2 pounds potatoes, peeled	3 tablespoons finely chopped
and cut into large chunks	fresh flat-leaf parsley
1 medium-sized red onion,	3 tablespoons olive oil
peeled and thinly sliced	1 1/2 tablespoons red
1/3 cup capers, rinsed	wine vinegar
	Salt
	Freshly ground black pepper

Boil the potatoes and drain in a colander. Transfer to a large bowl and combine with all the other ingredients, seasoning the salad with salt and pepper. Serve while the potatoes are still warm. [SERVES 4]

STUFFED KOHLRABI

Kohlrabi, turnips and celery root are popular winter vegetables, often added to meat stews or stuffed as in this hearty dish.

6 baseball-sized kohlrabi	Small handful finely chopped
FOR THE STUFFING:	fresh flat-leaf parsley
2 tablespoons olive oil	4–5 sprigs fresh thyme
1 medium-sized yellow onion,	1/2 cup white wine
peeled and finely diced	Salt
2 cloves garlic, peeled	Freshly ground black pepper
and finely diced	2 cups béchamel sauce
12 ounces ground veal	(see page 152)
8 ounces mushrooms,	
finely diced	

Slice the tops off the kohlrabi and trim away the stalks and leaves. Carefully cut out the centers, making sure that the skins do not break. Dice the kohlrabi flesh and set aside. Cook the kohlrabi in a large saucepan of boiling salted water for 15 minutes or until softened. Drain and cool.

TO PREPARE THE STUFFING: heat the oil in a large skillet and sauté the onion and garlic until softened. Add the veal and brown, stirring constantly for 5 to 10 minutes. Add the mushrooms, the reserved diced kohlrabi, parsley, thyme and wine. Stir together, then simmer for 40 minutes or until the mixture has thickened. Remove from the heat, season to taste with salt and pepper, and allow to cool.

Preheat the oven to 400°F. Put the kohlrabi into a lightly oiled baking dish and pack with the stuffing mixture. Spoon the béchamel over the tops of the filled kohlrabi and bake for 30 minutes. Cover the tops with aluminium foil if the béchamel browns too quickly. Remove from the oven and serve hot. [SERVES 6]

LEFT: VEGETABLES À LA GRECQUE
RIGHT: POTATO, ONION AND CAPER SALAD

HALLOUMI, BANANA CHILES, CHERRY TOMATO AND ESCAROLE SALAD

Banana chiles are actually mild long green peppers. They are good added to salads either raw or cooked. Halloumi cheese from Cyprus is probably more popular overseas than in Greece. It is a fantastic cheese for broiling and frying.

- 2 tablespoons olive oil plus extra for drizzling
- 8 ounces banana chiles, seeds and membranes removed, cut into strips
- 8 ounces halloumi cheese, cut into slices
- 3 ounces escarole or alternative salad leaves
- 8 ounces cherry tomatoes, halved lengthwise
- 1 teaspoon dried oregano
- Salt
- Freshly ground black pepper

Heat the oil in a skillet over a medium heat. Add the chiles and sauté for 10 to 15 minutes or until softened. Remove from the pan. Add the halloumi slices to the same pan and sauté for about 2 to 3 minutes, or until golden brown.

To serve, place the escarole leaves, halloumi, cherry tomatoes and chiles on individual plates or into a large salad bowl. Sprinkle with the oregano, season with salt and pepper, and drizzle with a little extra olive oil. [SERVES 4]

ZUCCHINI FLOWERS STUFFED WITH SOFT CHEESE AND RED PEPPERS

Apart from the common Cretan stuffing of rice, zucchini flowers are also stuffed with cheese and peppers and baked in the oven.

- 16 zucchini flowers

FOR THE FILLING:
- 5 tablespoons soft mizithra or ricotta cheese
- 1 red bell pepper, seeds and membranes removed, finely chopped
- 1 small red onion, peeled and finely chopped
- 1 tablespoon finely chopped fresh dill
- Salt
- Freshly ground black pepper
- 1 tablespoon olive oil

Preheat the oven to 350 °F. In a bowl, combine all the filling ingredients. Trim the stems of the zucchini flowers and stuff each flower with 1 to 2 teaspoons of the filling. Do not overstuff the flowers. Fold over the petals of each to secure the filling. Place in an ovenproof dish and pour enough water around the zucchini flowers to just begin to come up their sides. Bake for 20 to 30 minutes or until tender. Serve warm. [SERVES 4]

LEFT: HALLOUMI, BANANA CHILES, CHERRY TOMATO AND ESCAROLE SALAD
FOLLOWING PAGES: (LEFT) BRIAM / BAKED EGGPLANT, ZUCCHINI AND POTATOES (PAGE 52) (RIGHT) FASOLIA YIACHNI / STEWED YELLOW BEANS, POTATOES AND TOMATOES

GRATIN OF ZUCCHINI, TOMATOES AND POTATOES

Seasonal vegetables such as eggplant, peppers and zucchini are frequently combined with potatoes, tomatoes and herbs. Baked in the oven or stewed in one pot, they are especially delicious when cooked slowly in a wood-fired oven.

- 4 medium-sized potatoes, peeled and thinly sliced
- 3 tomatoes, thinly sliced
- 8 zucchini, trimmed and thinly sliced
- Salt
- Freshly ground black pepper
- 2 garlic cloves, peeled and minced
- 2 tablespoons olive oil
- 3 tablespoons breadcrumbs

Preheat the oven to 400°F. Place the potatoes, tomatoes and zucchini in alternate layers in a 10-inch round, 1 1/2-inch deep ovenproof dish, seasoning each layer with salt, pepper and garlic. Drizzle half the olive oil over the top layer, sprinkle the breadcrumbs over the top and drizzle with the remaining olive oil. Bake for 40 minutes or until the top has browned and the vegetables are tender. [SERVES 4]

FASOLIA YIACHNI / STEWED YELLOW BEANS, POTATOES AND TOMATOES

Yiachni is a Turkish word for vegetable or meat medleys that have been stewed in a pot. In Greece, many vegetables, such as beans, eggplants, artichokes, potatoes and cauliflower, benefit from this method of slow cooking with olive oil and herbs. In many island homes, where meat is used sparingly, these dishes constitute a main meal, served with the addition of some feta cheese. They are also delicious when reheated.

- 2 tablespoons olive oil
- 1 medium-sized yellow onion, peeled and chopped
- 3 tomatoes, peeled and chopped
- 2 cloves garlic, peeled and finely diced
- 2 pounds yellow wax beans or alternatively green beans
- 2 pounds potatoes, peeled and quartered
- 2–3 bay leaves
- 1 teaspoon dried oregano
- 1 tablespoon tomato paste
- Salt
- Freshly ground black pepper

TO SERVE:
- 1 tablespoon finely chopped fresh flat-leaf parsley

Heat the oil in a large saucepan over medium heat and sauté all the ingredients, except the yellow beans and potatoes, for 10 minutes.

Add the yellow beans and potatoes and continue to cook, stirring well, for 5 minutes. Add enough water to just cover the mixture and simmer for 45 minutes until the sauce has thickened. Season to taste with salt and pepper. Serve either hot or cold sprinkled with the parsley. [SERVES 6]

BRIAM / BAKED EGGPLANT, ZUCCHINI AND POTATOES

Briam is a popular summertime medley of baked vegetables. Add other ingredients, such as peppers, okra and carrot for even more variety.

3 tablespoons olive oil	5 tomatoes, thinly sliced
1 large eggplant, thinly sliced	6 zucchini, trimmed and
1 large onion, peeled and	thinly sliced
thinly sliced	Salt
2 garlic cloves, peeled	Freshly ground black pepper
and diced	1 teaspoon dried oregano
2 large potatoes, peeled and	$1/2$ cup water
thinly sliced	3 tablespoons breadcrumbs

Preheat the oven to 400°F. Heat 1 tablespoon of the oil in a skillet over medium heat. Add the eggplant, onion and garlic and sauté for 5 to 7 minutes or until softened. Place in a 12-by-12-by-2-inch baking dish. Place the potatoes, tomatoes and zucchini in alternate layers on top of the eggplant and onion mixture, seasoning each layer with salt, pepper and oregano. Pour the water and drizzle 1 tablespoon oil over the top layer of zucchini. Sprinkle over the breadcrumbs and drizzle with the remaining tablespoon of oil. Bake for 45 minutes or until the top has browned and the vegetables are tender. [SERVES 4]

MELITZANES STO FOURNO / BAKED EGGPLANT WITH TOMATO AND CHEESE

Eggplants are also stuffed with this meatless filling. It makes a delicious summertime dish when served cold.

4 tablespoons olive oil	1 twelve-ounce can peeled
2 medium-sized yellow onions,	tomatoes, finely chopped
peeled and finely chopped	1 tablespoon tomato paste
2 cloves garlic, peeled and	Salt
finely chopped	Freshly ground black pepper
1 handful finely chopped fresh	6 long thin eggplants
flat-leaf parsley	$1/2$ cup grated kefalotiri or
1 teaspoon dried oregano	parmesan cheese

Preheat the oven to 350°F. Heat half the olive oil in a saucepan and sauté the onion, garlic, parsley and oregano for 5 minutes or until softened. Stir in the tomatoes, tomato paste and enough water to just cover the mixture, and simmer for 30 minutes. Season to taste with salt and pepper. Halve the eggplants lengthways, score the flesh in a crisscross pattern with a sharp knife, then scoop out most of the flesh and discard. Rinse the eggplants in water, then pat dry with paper towels. Heat the remaining oil in a skillet and sauté the eggplants for 5 to 7 minutes, turning once. Drain on paper towels and place on a lightly oiled baking sheet. Fill each eggplant with the tomato mixture and sprinkle cheese over the top. Bake for 30 minutes or until golden brown on top. Serve hot or cold. [SERVES 4–6]

PAPOUTSAKIA

This dish takes its name from the "little shoes" that the stuffed eggplants resemble when cooked. It is also possible to make this dish with Japanese thin eggplants or zucchini.

2 large eggplants,	2 cups béchamel sauce (see
stems cut off	page 152)
2 tablespoons olive oil	3 tablespoons breadcrumbs
2 cups meat sauce (see page	2 tablespoons grated kefalotiri
152)	or parmesan cheese

Halve the eggplants lengthways, score the flesh in a crisscross pattern with a sharp knife, then scoop out most of the flesh to allow room for the stuffing, being careful not to break the skin. Chop the eggplant flesh. Heat the oil in a large skillet over medium heat and sauté the eggplant flesh for 5 minutes or until softened. Add to the meat sauce and combine well.

Preheat the oven to 350°F. Add the eggplant halves to the skillet and sauté for 5 minutes or until softened, turning them once. Remove from the pan, drain on paper towels and place on a lightly oiled baking sheet. Fill the center of each eggplant with some of the meat mixture and then spread the béchamel sauce over the top. Sprinkle with the breadcrumbs and cheese. Bake for 45 minutes or until golden brown. Serve hot. [SERVES 4]

ARAKAS YIACHNI / STEWED PEAS

Similar dishes appear in tavernas whenever fresh peas are in season.

5 tablespoons olive oil	4 large tomatoes, peeled,
2 medium-sized yellow	seeded and finely chopped
onions, peeled and chopped	2 tablespoons finely chopped
3 cloves garlic, peeled and	fresh flat-leaf parsley
finely chopped	1 teaspoon dried mint
3 green onions, including	Salt
green stems, finely chopped	Freshly ground black pepper
1 teaspoon dried oregano	2 pounds fresh peas, shelled
2 tablespoons finely chopped	$1/2$ head romaine lettuce, finely
fresh mint	shredded
1 teaspoon sugar	

Heat the oil in a large saucepan over medium heat and sauté the onions, garlic, green onions, dried oregano and fresh mint for 10 minutes or until softened. Add the sugar, tomatoes, fresh parsley and dried mint, and simmer for a further 10 minutes. Season to taste with salt and pepper.

Add the peas and lettuce and continue to cook, stirring well, for 5 minutes. Add enough water to just cover the mixture and simmer for 20 minutes or until the sauce has thickened. Serve either hot or cold. [SERVES 6]

ZUCCHINI MOUSSAKA

This makes a good alternative to the heavy eggplants and potatoes traditionally used in moussaka.

3 tablespoons olive oil	4 cups meat sauce (see page 152)
2 pounds zucchini, trimmed and sliced lengthways	4 cups béchamel sauce (see page 152)
Salt	
Freshly ground black pepper	1 tablespoon grated kefalotiri or parmesan cheese
4 tablespoons breadcrumbs	

Preheat the oven to 350°F. Heat the olive oil in a skillet and sauté the zucchini slices, seasoning with salt and pepper and turning once, for 5 minutes or until golden brown. Transfer the vegetables to paper towels to drain.

Lightly oil a 9-by-9-inch square baking dish, and sprinkle half the breadcrumbs on the bottom. Lay half the zucchini slices on top of the breadcrumbs and cover with half the meat sauce. Add the remaining zucchini slices on top and spread with the remaining meat sauce. Spread the béchamel sauce evenly over this mixture and sprinkle with the remaining breadcrumbs and cheese. Bake for 40 minutes. Cut into squares and serve warm. [SERVES 6]

ANGINARES ME ARAKA / STEWED ARTICHOKES AND PEAS

Artichokes make their way into many dishes. They are especially good stuffed with meat and topped with béchamel or slow-cooked with lamb and served with avgolemono sauce. In this dish artichokes are stewed with peas and mint.

8 fresh artichoke hearts with stems trimmed, quartered	6 tomatoes, peeled, seeded and finely chopped
3 tablespoons olive oil	3 tablespoons finely chopped fresh mint
1 medium-sized yellow onion, peeled and sliced	1 pound fresh peas, shelled
1 garlic clove, peeled and finely diced	Salt
	Freshly ground black pepper

Place the artichoke hearts in a bowl of acidulated water until ready to use. Heat the oil in a large saucepan over medium heat and sauté the onion and garlic for 10 minutes or until softened. Add the tomatoes and mint and simmer for another 10 minutes. Add the peas and drained artichokes and continue to cook, stirring well, for 5 minutes. Season to taste with salt and pepper. Add enough water to just cover the mixture and simmer for 20 minutes or until the sauce has thickened. Serve either hot or cold. [SERVES 4]

LEFT: ZUCCHINI MOUSSAKA
ABOVE (FROM FRONT):
ANGINARES ME ARAKA / STEWED ARTICHOKES AND PEAS
ANGINARES A LA POLITA / ARTICHOKES IN THE CONSTANTINOPLE STYLE

ANGINARES A LA POLITA / ARTICHOKES IN THE CONSTANTINOPLE STYLE

This popular dish takes its name from the polis *(city) of Constantinople, as Greeks still affectionately call modern-day Istanbul. It is found in tavernas everywhere whenever artichokes are in season in the spring and autumn.*

8 fresh artichoke hearts with stems trimmed, whole or halved	2 bay leaves
	1 1/2 tablespoons finely chopped fresh dill including stems
3 tablespoons olive oil	Salt
12 shallots or baby onions, peeled whole	Freshly ground black pepper
4–5 medium-sized red waxy potatoes, quartered	FOR THE AVGOLEMONO SAUCE:
	2 eggs, lightly beaten
2 carrots, peeled and sliced	Juice of 1 1/2 lemons

Place the artichoke hearts in a bowl of acidulated water until ready to use. Heat the oil in a large saucepan over medium heat and sauté the shallots for 5 minutes or until softened. Add the potatoes and carrots and sauté for another 10 minutes.

Add the drained artichokes, bay leaves and dill and continue to cook, stirring well, for 5 minutes. Add enough water to just cover the mixture and simmer for 30 to 40 minutes or until the sauce has thickened. Season to taste with salt and pepper.

TO MAKE THE AVGOLEMONO SAUCE: whisk the eggs and lemon juice together in a bowl. Take some of the liquid from the saucepan and slowly whisk into the avgolemono mixture. Stir this mixture slowly back into the saucepan over a low heat, shaking the pan until the sauce begins to thicken. Remove immediately from the heat and serve warm. [SERVES 4]

GRAINS + PULSES + PASTA

PULSES HAVE ALWAYS PLAYED AN INTEGRAL ROLE IN GREECE. FAVA BEANS, SPLIT PEAS, CHICKPEAS AND LENTILS WERE WIDELY EATEN BY THE ANCIENT GREEKS; IN FACT, THEIR RECIPE FOR *FAKI* (LENTIL SOUP) REMAINS UNCHANGED TODAY. IT IS STILL EATEN IN THE WINTER MONTHS, SIMMERED WITH ONIONS, HERBS AND OLIVE OIL AND FINISHED OFF WITH A SPLASH OF RED WINE VINEGAR. WHEN COLUMBUS BROUGHT NEW WORLD VEGETABLES SUCH AS BEANS AND TOMATOES BACK TO EUROPE, THEY RAPIDLY ESTABLISHED A FIRM FOOTHOLD IN GREECE.

Poverty and religion—particularly the 40 fasting days of *Sarakosti* (Lent)— have ensured the enduring popularity of the New World beans in their dried form. Easy to grow, they have enriched the country's peasant cuisine with satisfying recipes such as *fassoulada* (bean soup), *gigantes* (baked lima beans) and *mavromatika me seskoula* (black-eyed beans with chard).

Grains are also important. Two types of pasta, *hilopittes* (egg noodles) and *kritharaki* (orzo), are usually added to roasts and stews, where they absorb the cooking liquids. Spaghetti with tomato or meat sauce is as commonplace as it is in Italy. Rich *pastitsio* (meat and pasta pie) is available in every taverna. *Pligouri* (bulgur wheat) and *trachanas* (dried sour milk and flour pasta) are used to thicken soups and stews. Rice is used to stuff vegetables, squid, meatballs and fritters. Combined with seasonal vegetables, rice is also eaten year-round as a main course in four easy-to-make recipes: *spanakorizo* (spinach rice), *lachanorizo* (cabbage rice), *prassorizo* (leek rice) and *domatorizo* (tomato rice). All are also served as a side dish to many meat and fish dishes.

TAHINOSOUPA (PAGE 60)

SPANAKORIZO / SPINACH RICE

One-pot rice and vegetable medleys are made throughout the year. The most common are made with spinach, cabbage, leeks or tomatoes. Seasonal horta *(wild greens) and vegetables are also added in many rural parts of Greece.*

4 tablespoons olive oil	1 tablespoon dried oregano
4 green onions, including green stems, finely chopped	1 tablespoon dried mint
2 cloves garlic, peeled and finely chopped	2 pounds spinach, including stems, washed and roughly chopped
1/3 cup long-grain white rice, washed	Salt
3 tablespoons finely chopped fresh dill including stems	Freshly ground black pepper

Heat half the olive oil in a large saucepan over medium heat and sauté the green onions and garlic for about 5 minutes or until softened. Add the rice, dill and dried herbs and sauté for another 2 minutes. Add enough water to just cover the ingredients, then add the spinach and stir constantly until it wilts. Then, add the remaining 2 tablespoons of olive oil, salt and pepper to taste and, if necessary, enough water to just cover the mixture. Simmer for 15 to 20 minutes or until the rice is cooked and most of the liquid has been absorbed, stirring occasionally to prevent the mixture from sticking to the pan. At the end, if the mixture is too liquid, remove the saucepan from the heat, stretch a thick tea towel over the pan and replace the lid (the cloth will absorb any extra moisture). Set aside for a few minutes and then serve. [SERVES 4–6]

TRACHANOSOUPA
TRACHANAS AND TOMATO SOUP

In Greek villages, trachanas *(a dried pebble-like pasta made from sour milk and flour) is laid out on linen cloths to dry on rooftops in the hot summer months. This ancient staple was eaten by shepherds as they moved their flocks around the Balkans. It is delicious fried or added as a thickening agent to simple vegetable soups. Trachanas is available at speciality Greek or Middle Eastern delicatessens; otherwise substitute bulgur wheat.*

2/3 cup trachanas	Salt
3 tablespoons olive oil	Freshly ground black pepper
1 cup basic tomato sauce (see page 152)	3/4 cup grated kefalotiri or parmesan cheese

Place the trachanas and olive oil in a saucepan. Cover with water and bring to a boil, then simmer for 10 minutes. Add the tomato sauce, season with salt and pepper, and simmer for 20 minutes or until the soup has thickened. Serve in bowls with some grated cheese. [SERVES 4]

DOMATORIZO / TOMATO RICE

4 tablespoons olive oil	1 tablespoon finely chopped fresh marjoram
2 white onions, peeled and thinly sliced	5 Roma tomatoes, quartered
2 cloves garlic, peeled and finely chopped	Salt
1 cup long-grain white rice, washed	Freshly ground black pepper

Heat half the olive oil in a large saucepan over medium heat and sauté the onions and garlic for about 5 minutes or until softened. Add the rice and marjoram and sauté for 2 minutes more. Add enough water to just cover the ingredients, then add the tomatoes and stir well. Then, add the remaining 2 tablespoons of olive oil, salt and pepper to taste and, if necessary, enough water to just cover the mixture. Simmer for 15 to 20 minutes or until the rice is cooked and most of the liquid has been absorbed, stirring occasionally to prevent the mixture from sticking to the pan. At the end, if the mixture is too liquid, remove the saucepan from the heat, stretch a thick tea towel over the pan and replace the lid (the cloth will absorb any extra moisture). Set aside for a few minutes and then serve. [SERVES 4]

REVITHIA PADREMENA
CHICKPEA AND ORZO SOUP

Chickpeas with orzo, pasta or rice are a favorite combination throughout the Mediterranean. In Greece, as in Spain and Italy, they are usually cooked simply with one vital vegetable, herb or spice added, such as spinach, garlic, saffron, rosemary or hot peppers.

2 1/4 cups dried chickpeas	1 tablespoon fresh rosemary
2 tablespoons olive oil	Salt
Scant 1 cup orzo	Freshly ground black pepper

Cover chickpeas with cold water in a bowl and soak for at least 1 hour or overnight. Drain and place in a saucepan. Cover with cold water, add the olive oil and bring to the boil. Then simmer for 1 1/2 hours or until tender. Add the orzo and rosemary and cook for a further 10 minutes or until the orzo is al dente. Season to taste with salt and pepper, adding a little more water if the mixture is too thick, and serve. [SERVES 4]

FAKI / LENTIL SOUP

Puy lentils are preferable for their delicate flavor. However, in Greece, brown lentils, despite their longer cooking time, have been used in similar soups since ancient times.

1 1/4	cups lentils, washed and picked over for stones	2	bay leaves
2	garlic cloves, peeled and diced	6	tablespoons olive oil
1	celery stalk, finely diced		Salt
1	medium-sized red onion, peeled and diced		Freshly ground black pepper
1	large russet potato, peeled and diced		**TO SERVE:**
		2	slices sourdough bread, crusts removed, cubed
			Red wine vinegar

Place the lentils, garlic, celery, onion, potato, bay leaves and 2 tablespoons of the olive oil in a saucepan. Cover with water and bring to a boil, then simmer for 30 minutes or until the lentils are cooked. Season with salt and pepper.

To serve, prepare croutons by sautéing the bread cubes in the remaining 4 tablespoons of olive oil until golden brown, then drain on paper towels. Ladle the soup into bowls with the croutons and a splash of red wine vinegar. [SERVES 4]

TAHINOSOUPA

In Greece, tahini (sesame seed paste) is frequently eaten during the Lenten fast. It is mainly used in soups, pies and dips.

4	cups water, plus 3 tablespoons	1/2	cup tahini
1/3	cup long-grain white rice, washed		Juice of 2 lemons
			Salt
			Freshly ground black pepper

Bring the 4 cups water to a boil in a saucepan. Add the rice and simmer for 15 minutes or until tender. In a small bowl, beat the tahini, lemon juice and 3 tablespoons of cold water together. Add this mixture to the rice, stir well and simmer for 5 minutes more. Season with salt and pepper and serve. [SERVES 4]

YOUVARLAKIA / VEAL AND RICE BALLS WITH AVGOLEMONO SAUCE

This popular dish can be found in tavernas throughout Greece. When served as a soup, other vegetables, such as carrot, celery and onion, are sometimes added to the pot.

1	pound ground veal	3	tablespoons olive oil
1	large yellow onion, peeled and grated		Salt
1/4	cup long-grain white rice, washed		Freshly ground black pepper
2	tablespoons finely chopped fresh flat-leaf parsley		**FOR THE AVGOLEMONO SAUCE:**
			Juice of 1 lemon
		2	eggs, lightly beaten

Mix the veal, onion, rice, parsley, 1 tablespoon of the olive oil, salt and pepper in a large bowl, kneading together until blended. Roll the mixture into balls just smaller than golf balls (if too large or small they will break up when cooking). Refrigerate until ready to use.

Bring some water and the remaining 2 tablespoons olive oil to a boil in a large saucepan (there should be enough water to just cover the veal and rice balls when immersed). Lower the heat and carefully add the veal and rice balls into the saucepan. Simmer for 30 minutes or until cooked. Remove the saucepan from the heat.

TO MAKE THE AVGOLEMONO SAUCE: mix the lemon juice and eggs together in a bowl and whisk in a ladleful of the cooking liquid from the saucepan. Pour the mixture over the veal and rice balls, then return the pot to the heat for a few minutes, shaking the pot back and forth until the sauce begins to thicken. Transfer the veal and rice balls to bowls, pour over the sauce and serve immediately. [SERVES 4]

LEFT: FAKI / LENTIL SOUP
RIGHT: YOUVARLAKIA / VEAL AND RICE BALLS WITH AVGOLEMONO SAUCE

PLIGOURI SALATA / BULGUR WHEAT SALAD

Bulgur or burghul (cracked wheat), as it is variously called, is widely used in northern Greece and Crete in stews, pies, vegetable stuffings and salads.

1^1/$_3$ cups bulgur wheat	^{3}/$_4$ cup olive oil
4 green onions, including green stems, finely chopped	Juice of 2 lemons
	Salt
4 tablespoons roughly chopped fresh mint	Freshly ground black pepper

Place the bulgur wheat in a bowl and cover with cold water. Leave for 30 minutes or until the wheat begins to swell and soften, then drain and squeeze out any excess water. Combine the bulgur wheat with the green onions, mint, olive oil and lemon juice. Season to taste with salt and pepper. Stir the mixture well and marinate for 30 minutes in the refrigerator. [SERVES 4]

MAVROMATIKA PIAZ / BLACK-EYED PEA SALAD

Laced with plenty of olive oil and vinegar, black-eyed peas are combined with vegetables and herbs to make filling salads.

1^1/$_4$ cups dried black-eyed peas	4 tablespoons finely chopped fresh flat-leaf parsley with stems
2 Roma tomatoes, peeled and diced	5 tablespoons olive oil
8 ounces Yukon gold potatoes, peeled, diced and boiled	3 tablespoons red wine vinegar
	Salt
	Freshly ground black pepper

Place the peas in a large saucepan, cover with water and simmer for 30 minutes or until tender. Be careful not to overcook, as they become mushy. Drain and allow to cool. Combine with all the other ingredients in a bowl, and season to taste with salt and pepper. Stir the mixture well and marinate for 30 minutes in the refrigerator. [SERVES 4]

FAKES SALATA / LENTIL SALAD

Lentils are often combined with pasta and rice or eaten cold in simple summer salads.

1^1/$_2$ cups Puy lentils, washed and picked over for stones	Salt
	Freshly ground black pepper
2 bay leaves	1 medium-sized red onion, peeled and thinly sliced
8 tablespoons olive oil	
Juice of 2 oranges	1 orange, peeled and cut into segments

Place the lentils, bay leaves and 2 tablespoons of the olive oil in a saucepan. Cover with water and bring to a boil, then simmer for 20 minutes or until the lentils are cooked. Drain in a colander and allow to cool. Place in a serving bowl. Add the orange juice and remaining 6 tablespoons of olive oil, and season with salt and pepper. Stir the mixture well and marinate for 30 minutes in the refrigerator. Just before serving, mix in the sliced onion and orange segments. [SERVES 4]

PHAKOS KE PRASSON / LENTIL AND LEEK SOUP

Mention is made by Athenaeus of a similar soup in ancient Greece. I tried this out one year at my Greek cooking school and it was a great success. We ate it when it cooled down and all the flavors had time to develop.

2^1/$_2$ cups lentils	1 teaspoon dried pennyroyal
4 large leeks, trimmed and sliced	1 teaspoon dried mint
	1 teaspoon fresh rosemary
3 tablespoons olive oil	1 tablespoon honey
1 teaspoon coriander seeds	1 tablespoon red wine vinegar
1 teaspoon fennel seeds	^{1}/$_2$ cup white wine

Place the lentils, leeks and olive oil in a large saucepan. Cover with water and simmer for 30 minutes or until tender. In a mortar, grind the coriander, fennel, pennyroyal, mint and rosemary to a paste with a pestle. Moisten with a little liquid from the lentil and leek soup. Add the honey, vinegar and wine to the mortar. Stir the mixture back into the saucepan and simmer for 10 minutes. Allow to cool and serve either hot or cold. [SERVES 6–8]

CLOCKWISE FROM FRONT:
PLIGOURI SALATA / BULGUR WHEAT SALAD
MAVROMATIKA PIAZ / BLACK-EYED PEA SALAD
FAKES SALATA / LENTIL SALAD

MAVROMATIKA ME SESKOULA
BLACK-EYED PEA AND CHARD STEW

Swiss chard (silverbeet) is a common winter vegetable in Greece. It is delicious added as a filling in savory pies or as the starring ingredient in a slow-cooked stew.

3/4 cup dried black-eyed peas	6 Roma tomatoes, peeled and chopped
12 ounces Swiss chard, including stems	1 tablespoon tomato paste
3 tablespoons olive oil	Salt
3 garlic cloves, peeled and finely chopped	Freshly ground black pepper

Soak the black-eyed peas in cold water overnight, then drain. Wash the Swiss chard and trim the stems. Roughly chop the stems and leaves. Place the black-eyed peas and chard in a large saucepan, cover with water and simmer for 20 minutes or until almost tender. Drain in a colander, reserving 1 cup of the cooking liquid. Meanwhile, heat the oil in a skillet over medium heat. Add the garlic and sauté for 5 minutes or until softened. Add the tomatoes and sauté for a few more minutes. Add the black-eyed peas and chard, reserved cooking liquid and tomato paste. Stir the mixture well, season with salt and pepper, and simmer for about 20 minutes. Serve warm with bread and feta cheese.

[SERVES 4]

FASSOULADA / GREEK BEAN SOUP

This classic Greek vegetarian soup is simple to make. Served with plenty of crusty bread, it makes a perfect dish for a large impromptu party.

1 pound dried white beans, soaked overnight	2 tablespoons tomato paste
1 large yellow onion, peeled and roughly chopped	5 tablespoons olive oil
3 carrots, peeled and sliced	2 bay leaves
3 sticks celery, strings removed and sliced	A handful fresh flat-leaf parsley leaves
3 ripe tomatoes, peeled, seeded and roughly chopped (or 1 fifteen-ounce can peeled tomatoes)	Salt
	Freshly ground black pepper

Drain the beans and place in a large saucepan. Cover with cold water and bring to a boil, skimming off any froth with a slotted spoon. Add all the other ingredients except the seasonings, and simmer for 1 1/2 hours or until tender. Allow to cool slightly, season with salt and pepper, and ladle into bowls.

[SERVES 6–8]

LEFT: FASSOULADA / GREEK BEAN SOUP
ABOVE: MAVROMATIKA ME SESKOULA /
BLACK-EYED PEA AND CHARD STEW

ABOVE: PASTA WITH SPINACH, PARSLEY AND YOGURT
RIGHT: PASTITSIO / MEAT AND PASTA PIE

PASTITSIO / MEAT AND PASTA PIE

This famous baked meat and pasta pie is found throughout Greece. Although time-consuming to make, if made the day before and reheated in the oven, it is a great party dish.

FOR THE PASTA:

- 1 pound ziti
- 2 eggs, lightly beaten
- 3 tablespoons grated kefalotiri or parmesan cheese
- 1 cup béchamel sauce (see page 152)

FOR THE PIE:

- 2 tablespoons butter, melted
- 5 cups meat sauce (see page 152)
- 3 cups béchamel sauce (see page 152)
- 3 tablespoons breadcrumbs
- 3 tablespoons grated kefalotiri or parmesan cheese

TO PREPARE THE PASTA: bring a large saucepan of salted water to a boil. Add the pasta and simmer for 10 minutes or until almost soft. Drain in a colander and transfer to a large bowl. Allow to cool and then add the beaten eggs, cheese and béchamel sauce. Toss the pasta until well coated with the mixture.

TO ASSEMBLE THE PIE: preheat the oven to 350°F. Brush the bottom and sides of a rectangular 9-by-13-inch baking dish with the melted butter. Spread a third of the pasta evenly in the dish and cover with half of the meat sauce. Add another third of the pasta and cover with the remaining meat sauce. Spread the remaining pasta over top and spoon on the béchamel sauce, smoothing it over the top. Sprinkle on the breadcrumbs and cheese. Bake for 40 minutes or until the top is golden brown. Leave to rest for 10 minutes before cutting and serving. [MAKES 12 PORTIONS]

PASTA WITH SPINACH, PARSLEY AND YOGURT

This is a quick and easy meal to prepare. It is also a refreshing alternative to the usual Greek ways of serving pasta with tomato or meat sauce.

- 1 pound short pasta, such as macaroni
- 1 small bunch fresh spinach, washed and roughly chopped
- 2 tablespoons olive oil
- 3 tablespoons chopped fresh flat-leaf parsley with stems
- Salt
- Freshly ground black pepper
- 1 cup Greek-style yogurt

Bring a large saucepan of salted water to a boil. Add the pasta and spinach and simmer until pasta is tender. Drain in a colander and reserve 1/2 cup of the cooking liquid. Heat the oil in a large skillet and sauté the parsley for a few minutes. Add the pasta and spinach, season with salt and pepper, and sauté for 5 minutes, stirring well. Serve with a dollop of yogurt. [SERVES 4]

PIES + BREAD + PASTRIES

PSOMI (BREAD) IS INDISPENSABLE TO THE GREEK TABLE, AND EVERY VILLAGE AND CITY NEIGHBORHOOD ALWAYS HAS SEVERAL BAKERIES.

However overworked the baker might be, there will be several types of hot bread coming out of the oven during the day—perhaps some *eliopsomo* (olive bread), *tiropsomo* (cheese bread) *or bobota* (corn bread) in among the regular loaves of *horiatiko psomi* (country-style bread), *paximadia* (dried rusks) and cookies. On the busy streets of the cities and towns, *koulouria* (braided bread and sesame rings), *tiropites* (cheese pies) and *spanakopites* (spinach pies) are the universal street food. Festive breads such as *prosforo* (church bread), *tsoureki* (Easter bread), *christopsomo* (Christmas bread) and *vasilopita* (New Year's bread) are also sold in season. In city bakeries, the range of these fresh loaves, dried savory biscuits and sweet cookies is often astounding—an indication, if any were needed, of the rich baking traditions inherited from the ancient Greeks.

The country's *pites* (pies) are equally diverse. Savory pies of different shapes and sizes, made with fine layers of filo or a pastry crust, are usually filled with herbs, cheese and vegetables or meat. On the mainland, especially in northern Epirus, Macedonia and Thrace, where meat and vegetables are sometimes more plentiful than on the islands, there are some delicious and unusual combinations: *hortopites* (wild greens and herb pies), *prassopites* (leek and pepper pies) and *melitzanopites* (eggplant pies). In Cephalonia, the largest Ionian island, they also make *kefalonitiki kreatopita*, a rich meat and vegetable pie that is a legacy of the island's occupation by the Venetians.

SKALTSOUNIA / FRIED FENNEL PASTRIES AND
TIGANOPSOMO / FRIED CHEESE PASTRIES (PAGE 70)

SPANAKOPITA

Spinach pie is the universal snack in Greece, bought at bakeries and snack shops everywhere. These pies are often eaten on the run on the way to work or to stem mid-morning hunger before lunch, which is usually taken late in most parts of the country.

1 package commercial
  filo pastry
  Melted butter or olive oil
  to brush on the filo

FOR THE FILLING:
2 pounds fresh spinach,
  washed, trimmed and
  roughly chopped

8 green onions, including
  green stems, finely chopped
4 tablespoons finely chopped
  fresh dill
12 ounces feta cheese,
  crumbled
2 eggs, beaten
  Salt
  Freshly ground black pepper
1 tablespoon olive oil

TO PREPARE THE FILLING: blanch the spinach in boiling water, drain thoroughly, remove to a bowl and allow to cool. Add all the other ingredients and combine well.

TO ASSEMBLE THE PIE: preheat the oven to 350°F. Unwrap the filo pastry on a flat surface and cover with a damp tea towel. Lightly oil a 12-inch square baking dish. Place half the filo sheets in the bottom of the dish, brushing each sheet with the melted butter as it is added. Add all the filling and then spread the remaining filo sheets on top, brushing each one with the melted butter. Sprinkle a little water on top to prevent the filo from burning. Bake for 40 to 45 minutes or until the top is golden brown. Eat either hot or cold.

[SERVES 6]

TIGANOPSOMO / FRIED CHEESE PASTRIES

These pastries can be made in a variety of shapes. Always fried, they are best made with a very simple filling of feta cheese combined with some dried herbs.

1 quantity filo pastry (see
  page 153)

FOR THE FILLING:
1 tablespoon dried mint

10 ounces feta cheese,
  crumbled
  Olive oil for frying

Roll filo pastry thinly. Sprinkle with the mint and crumbled feta. Cut into small squares and then roughly fold the squares over, pressing the edges together to seal. Pour olive oil into a frying pan to a depth of 3/4 inch. Heat and, when hot, fry the pastries for about 4 to 5 minutes or until golden brown. Drain on paper towels and serve hot or lukewarm.

[MAKES 8–10 PASTRIES]

SKALTSOUNIA / FRIED FENNEL PASTRIES

In Crete, most families make these small pastries (also called kallitsounia*) on a regular basis. They are made in a variety of different shapes with different seasonal fillings — some wild greens just picked from the field, ripe tomatoes or diced eggplants, almost always sautéed with onion, cheese and herbs.*

1 quantity filo pastry (see
  page 153)
  Olive oil for frying

FOR THE FILLING:
1 tablespoon olive oil
3/4 cup finely chopped fennel
  bulb and leaves
1 small yellow onion, peeled
  and finely chopped

3 tablespoons grated
  kefalotiri or parmesan
  cheese
1 tablespoon finely chopped
  fresh flat-leaf parsley
  Salt
  Freshly ground black pepper

TO PREPARE THE FILLING: heat the oil in a frying pan over medium heat. Add the fennel and onion and sauté for 5 minutes or until softened. Remove to a bowl and allow to cool. Add the cheese and parsley, and season to taste with salt and pepper.

Roll filo pastry thinly. Using a circular cookie cutter approximately 5 inches in diameter, cut the pastry into circles. Place 1 tablespoon of filling in the middle of each circle, then fold the pastry over the filling. Press the edges together and seal by pinching the pastry with fingertips or a fork. Pour olive oil into a frying pan to a depth of 3/4 inch. Heat and, when hot, fry the pastries for about 4 to 5 minutes or until golden brown. Drain on paper towels and serve hot or lukewarm. [MAKES 10–12 PASTRIES]

KOTOPITA / CHICKEN PIE

Chicken pies are more often found on mainland Greece. The meat is combined with other ingredients, such as red peppers, feta cheese or onions, as in this recipe from Epirus.

1 quantity basic pastry (see page 153)

FOR THE FILLING:

2 tablespoons olive oil

4 small white onions, peeled and sliced

1 pound chicken, cooked and shredded

1/4 cup grated kefalotiri or parmesan cheese

3 eggs, beaten

1 teaspoon dried mint

1 teaspoon grated nutmeg

1/2 teaspoon ground allspice

1/2 teaspoon finely chopped fresh marjoram

Salt

Freshly ground black pepper

FOR THE GLAZE:

1 egg yolk

2 tablespoons milk

TO PREPARE THE FILLING: heat the oil in a skillet over medium heat. Add the onions and sauté for 5 minutes or until softened. Remove to a large bowl and allow to cool. Add all the other filling ingredients and combine well.

TO ASSEMBLE THE PIE: preheat oven to 350°F. Lightly oil a 9-inch round pie dish. Roll out the pastry on a lightly floured board to a thickness of 1/4 inch and loosely place in the baking tin so that the pastry covers the bottom and hangs over the sides. Place the filling in the pastry-lined baking tin and pull the remaining pastry over the filling to create a top to the pie, tucking and pinching any loose pastry bits into the sides. Prepare the glaze by whisking the egg yolk and milk together. Brush the pastry with the glaze and cut two vents in the middle of the pie to allow any steam to escape. Bake for 45 minutes or until the top is golden brown. Allow to cool. Serve either hot or cold, sliced in wedges. [SERVES 4–6]

KEFALONITIKI KREATOPITA CEPHALONIAN MEAT PIE

The Ionian islands were once part of the Venetian Empire. Cephalonia, the largest island in the group, is home to this festive, rich recipe, which owes much to the Baroque pies of northern Italy. This great party dish is eaten on feast days and family celebrations. Halve the ingredients for a smaller pie.

2 quantities of basic pastry (see page 153)

FOR THE FILLING:

2 tablespoons olive oil

1 medium-sized yellow onion, peeled and finely chopped

2 cloves garlic, peeled and finely diced

1 pound boned lamb leg or shoulder lamb, trimmed of fat, chopped in 1/4-inch dice

1 pound tip roast or round of beef trimmed of fat, chopped in 1/4-inch dice

1 medium-sized russet potato, peeled and cut in small cubes

1/4 cup long-grain white rice, parboiled

1/4 cup currants

1/4 cup grated kefalotiri or parmesan cheese

2 tomatoes, peeled and grated

1 tablespoon finely chopped fresh mint

1 tablespoon finely chopped fresh flat-leaf parsley

1 teaspoon finely chopped fresh marjoram

1 teaspoon powdered cinnamon

1/2 teaspoon dried oregano

1/4 cup red wine

Salt

Freshly ground black pepper

3 hard-boiled eggs, shelled and quartered

1/2 cup beef stock

FOR THE GLAZE:

1 egg yolk

2 tablespoons milk

TO PREPARE THE FILLING: heat the oil in a skillet over medium heat. Add the onion and garlic and sauté for 5 minutes or until softened. Remove to a large bowl. Sauté the lamb and beef in the skillet for 5 minutes or until browned. Remove to the bowl. Add all the other ingredients, except the hard-boiled eggs and stock. Mix well and refrigerate until ready to use. Allow to marinate for a few hours, or longer if possible.

TO ASSEMBLE THE PIE: preheat oven to 425°F. Lightly oil a 12-inch square baking dish. Roll out the 2 quantities of pastry separately on a lightly floured board to a thickness of 1/4 inch. Loosely place the first in the baking dish so that the pastry covers the bottom and hangs over the sides. Place the filling in the pastry-lined baking dish. Add the egg quarters around the filling and pour in the stock. Lay the other piece of pastry over the top of the pie, making sure that the sides of the pie are covered with pastry. Trim any remaining pastry away from the baking dish. Prepare the glaze by whisking the egg yolk and milk together. Brush the pastry with the glaze and cut two vents in the middle of the pie to allow any steam to escape. Bake at 425°F for 30 minutes and then lower heat to 350°F and bake for another 50 minutes or until the top is golden brown. Allow to cool. Serve either hot or cold, sliced in wedges. [SERVES 8–10]

RIGHT: KOTOPITA / CHICKEN PIE
FOLLOWING PAGES: (LEFT) KEFALONITIKI KREATOPITA/
CEPHALONIAN MEAT PIE
(RIGHT) SEAFOOD, FETA AND
RED PEPPER PIES (PAGE 76)

1 1/2 hours or until doubled in size. Preheat oven to 350°F. Knead again and then divide the dough in half if making into 2 loaves; otherwise divide into 12 pieces to make rolls. Shape pieces of dough into loaves or rolls. Place the loaves or rolls on oiled baking sheets and bake for 40 minutes or until the loaves or rolls are golden brown and give off a hollow sound when tapped. Eat either hot or cold. [MAKES ABOUT 12 ROLLS OR 2 LOAVES]

SEAFOOD, FETA AND RED PEPPER PIES

Although the Greeks don't really make fish pies very often, this recipe incorporates some typical Aegean flavors. Poach the fish and prawns with bay leaves, olive oil, onion and peppercorns.

1 package commercial filo pastry	1 large russet potato, peeled, boiled and diced
Melted butter or olive oil to brush on the filo	3 tablespoons finely chopped fresh flat-leaf parsley
FOR THE FILLING:	1 red bell pepper, seeds and membranes removed, finely chopped
1 pound cod or other meaty whitefish fillets, cooked	Salt
1 pound fresh prawns, shelled, deveined and cooked	Freshly ground black pepper
7 ounces feta, crumbled	1 tablespoon olive oil

Combine all the filling ingredients in a bowl and mix well.

TO ASSEMBLE THE PIES: preheat the oven to 350°F. Unwrap the filo pastry on a flat surface and cover with a damp tea towel. Lightly oil four round 5-Inch pie tins. Use one-fourth of the filo sheets from the package per pie. Place filo sheets in the first pie dish, brushing each sheet with the melted butter as it is added to the pie dish, ensuring that the filo hangs over the sides. Place about 4 tablespoons of filling in the pie and pull the overhanging filo over the filling to create a top to the pie, tucking and pinching any loose bits into the sides. Brush with melted butter or oil. Repeat the process with the remaining pies. Bake the pies for 15 minutes or until golden brown.

[MAKES 4 INDIVIDUAL PIES]

ELIOPSOMO / OLIVE BREAD

In Greece, bakeries often sell simple loaves enhanced with onions, dried herbs, olives or cheese. They are ideal snacks or light lunches when served with some hard cheese and ripe tomatoes.

1/2 ounce (2 packets) fast-acting dry yeast	5 tablespoons olive oil
1 teaspoon sugar	1 tablespoon dried mint
2 1/2 cups warm water	1 yellow onion, peeled and chopped
9 cups all-purpose flour	15 black olives, pitted and roughly chopped
4 teaspoons salt	

Dissolve the yeast, sugar and 1 1/2 cups of the water in a bowl. Combine the flour, salt and olive oil in a mixing bowl. Stir in the mint and onion. Add the yeast mixture and remaining 1 cup water, and mix into a dough. Turn onto a lightly floured surface and knead for 10 minutes. Add the olives and knead for a few more minutes. Place in a lightly oiled bowl, cover and leave for 1 to

ABOVE & RIGHT:
ELIOPSOMO / OLIVE BREAD

HORTOPITA / WILD GREENS PIE

The regions of Epirus and Crete are famed for savory pies using a huge variety of horta *(wild greens) and herbs. They are as nutritious as they are delicious.*

1 quantity basic pastry (see page 153)

FOR THE FILLING:

2 pounds mixed greens such as dandelion, mustard, chickweed, arugula, wild fennel, beet greens (alternatively use spinach, Swiss chard and a few fresh herbs)

2 medium-sized yellow onions, peeled and finely chopped

8 ounces feta cheese, crumbled

1/2 cup grated kefalotiri or parmesan cheese

3 eggs, beaten

1 tablespoon dried oregano

3 tablespoons finely chopped fresh mint

3 tablespoons olive oil

Salt

Freshly ground black pepper

Carefully rinse the greens, discarding any yellowed leaves or stems. Bring a large saucepan of salted water to a boil, put the greens and onions in the saucepan and simmer for 10 minutes. Drain and set aside to cool. Combine the greens with the remaining ingredients in a large bowl and season with salt and pepper to taste.

Preheat oven to 350°F. Lightly oil a 9-inch round pie tin. Roll out the pastry on a lightly floured board to a thickness of 1/4 inch and loosely place into the pie tin so that the pastry covers the bottom and hangs over the sides. Put the filling into the pastry-lined tin and pull the remaining pastry over the filling to create a top to the pie, tucking and pinching any loose pastry bits into the sides. Bake for 45 minutes or until the top is golden brown. Allow to cool. Serve either hot or cold, sliced in wedges. [SERVES 4–6]

TSOUREKI / GREEK EASTER BREAD

This famous festive Easter bread can be shaped a variety of ways. The most common loaf braids 3 ropes and adds red-dyed eggs. The braids are symbolic of the Holy Trinity; the eggs, of the blood of Christ and fertility.

1 1/2 cups milk

5 tablespoons butter

5 cups all-purpose flour

1 teaspoon salt

Zest of 1 orange

Scant 1/2 cup granulated sugar

1/4 ounce (1 packet) fast-acting dry yeast

3 tablespoons orange juice

2 eggs, beaten

FOR THE GLAZE:

3 tablespoons orange juice

2 tablespoons granulated sugar

2/3 cup almonds, slivered

Place the milk in a small saucepan and warm over low heat. Add the butter, stirring it into the milk as it melts, then allow to cool. Place 1 cup of the flour in a mixing bowl with the salt, orange zest and 1 teaspoon of the sugar.

Stir in the yeast, then beat in the butter and milk to make a batter. Cover and leave for 20 minutes until the mixture becomes bubbly. Then, add the remaining 4 cups flour, sugar, orange juice and eggs, and mix into a soft dough.

Turn onto a lightly floured surface and knead for 5 minutes. Place in a lightly oiled bowl, brush with a little melted butter, cover and leave for 1 to 1 1/2 hours or until doubled in size. Knead again and then divide the dough in half. Shape each piece into 3 ropes, each 12 inches long. Pinch the 3 ropes together at one end, then braid the 3 ropes into a plaited loaf. Repeat the process with the other 3 ropes. Place the 2 loaves on oiled baking sheets, cover and leave for 30 to 40 minutes or until doubled in size. Bake in a preheated oven at 375°F for 20 minutes.

Meanwhile, prepare the glaze. In a small saucepan, warm the orange juice over low heat. Add the sugar and stir to dissolve it into the orange juice. Remove the loaves from the oven and brush on the glaze. Sprinkle the slivered almonds on top of the loaves. Bake for 20 minutes more or until the loaves are golden brown and give off a hollow sound when tapped. Eat either hot or cold. [MAKES 2 LOAVES]

KOLOKITHOPITA

Whenever there is a surfeit of seasonal vegetables—zucchini in the summer or leeks in the winter—they tend to end up in savory pies. In northern Greece, meat or rice is also added for even heartier pies.

1 package commercial filo pastry

Melted butter or olive oil to brush on the filo

FOR THE FILLING:

1 1/2 pounds zucchini, washed and grated

10 ounces feta cheese, crumbled

3 tablespoons grated kefalotiri or parmesan cheese

8 green onions, including green stems, finely chopped

4 tablespoons finely chopped fresh dill

4 tablespoons finely chopped fresh mint

2 eggs, beaten

Salt

Freshly ground black pepper

2 tablespoon olive oil

TO PREPARE THE FILLING: let the zucchini sit in a colander, weighted down with a plate for 15 minutes, to remove some of its liquid. Then, place in a bowl, add all the other ingredients and combine well.

TO ASSEMBLE THE PIE: preheat the oven to 350°F. Unwrap the filo pastry on a flat surface and cover with a damp tea towel. Lightly oil a 12-inch square baking dish. Place half the filo sheets in the bottom of the dish, brushing each sheet with melted butter as it is added to the dish. Add all the filling and then spread the remaining filo sheets on top, brushing each one with the melted butter. Sprinkle a little water on top to prevent the filo from burning. Bake for 40 to 45 minutes or until the top is golden brown. Eat either hot or cold. [SERVES 6]

POULTRY + GAME

IN A COUNTRY WHERE LITTLE RED MEAT WAS EATEN, EXCEPT ON SPECIAL OCCASIONS, CHICKEN AND GAME WERE MAINSTAYS OF THE DIET IN MOST MOUNTAIN AND ISLAND VILLAGES. ONCE THEY HAD OUTLIVED THEIR USEFULNESS FOR EGG LAYING, HENS WERE SIMMERED IN A POT WITH VEGETABLES AND AROMATICS TO IMPROVE THEIR FLAVOR AND SOMETIMES TOUGH FLESH.

Today, chicken is widely available and it is difficult not to find a taverna serving slow-cooked one-pot chicken dishes such as *kapama* or *stifado*, combining chicken cuts with winter or summer vegetables, herbs and spices. Whole chickens, and *galopoula* (turkey) at Christmas, are also roasted and stuffed with nuts, raisins, bread and herbs, especially in the Cycladic and Dodecanese island groups.

Farmed quail, pheasant and duck are also available. During the start of the hunting season in early autumn, when many migrating birds leave northern Europe bound for Africa, wild game such as *fassianos* (pheasant), *bekatsa* (woodcock), *perdika* (partridge), *ortikia* (quail) and *agrioperistera* (pigeon) are hunted with abandon. They make their way into stews with the odd vegetable, herb or spice, or are simply grilled or pot-roasted and served with rice pilafs or pasta. In northern Greece, where game is plentiful, such dishes are widespread and inventively cooked in local homes.

CHICKEN BAKED IN YOGURT WITH SPINACH (PAGE 82)

CHICKEN BAKED IN YOGURT WITH SPINACH

Strained cow's or sheep's milk yogurt is often used as an ingredient in the northeast province of Thrace. Baked with herbs and spices, its texture becomes even thicker in this delicious and easy casserole.

2 tablespoons olive oil	3 tablespoons all-purpose flour
2 medium-sized yellow onions, peeled and sliced	2 teaspoons dried mint
4 chicken breasts on the bone	1 teaspoon ground cumin
2 pounds (4 cups) Greek-style thick yogurt, strained through cheesecloth	Salt
	Freshly ground black pepper
2 eggs, lightly beaten	2 tablespoons grated kefalotiri or parmesan cheese
2 cloves garlic, peeled and finely chopped	2 bunches fresh spinach, washed and steamed

Heat the olive oil in a large skillet and sauté the onions over medium heat until softened. Remove with a slotted spoon and set aside. Sauté the chicken breasts in the pan until browned, then transfer to an ovenproof dish with the onions.

Preheat the oven to 350°F. Put the yogurt in a large bowl and mix in the eggs, garlic, flour, mint, cumin, salt and pepper until well combined. Pour over the chicken, making sure that the mixture covers the chicken breasts. Sprinkle with the cheese and bake for 40 minutes or until the yogurt mixture has set and the chicken is tender. Serve with the steamed spinach on the side. [SERVES 4]

CHICKEN WITH ZUCCHINI, GREEN OLIVES AND GREEN GARLIC

This colorful stew is perfect for a summer lunch outdoors. Just add a simple green salad and chilled bottle of rosé wine.

3 tablespoons olive oil	8 zucchini, trimmed and thickly sliced
1 chicken approximately 4 pounds, cut into 6 pieces	4 Roma tomatoes, peeled and roughly chopped
2 red onions, peeled and roughly chopped	2 tablespoons chopped fresh flat-leaf parsley
4 stems green garlic, outer skin removed, trimmed and cut into 2 pieces (or 3 cloves garlic, peeled and diced)	Salt
	Freshly ground black pepper
	Juice of 1 lemon
	12 green olives, pits removed, rinsed in cold water

Heat the olive oil in a large saucepan and sauté the chicken pieces over medium heat until browned. Remove with a slotted spoon and set aside.

Sauté the onions and garlic in the saucepan until softened. Add the zucchini, tomatoes, parsley, salt and pepper and sauté for a further 10 minutes. Add the chicken pieces back into the saucepan. Add enough water to just cover the mixture and stir well. Simmer for 40 minutes, stirring occasionally. Add the lemon juice and olives and cook for another 15 minutes or until the sauce has thickened and the chicken is tender. Serve with rice or bread. [SERVES 4–6]

KOTOPOULO STIFADO / CHICKEN STEW

Stifado, the classic Greek stew that usually combines rabbit or veal with baby onions, wine and spices, can also be used with chicken or tuna. Such stews improve with flavor when reheated the next day and need little more than some crusty bread to mop up their thick sauces.

2 tablespoons olive oil	and finely chopped
2 pounds shallots or baby onions, peeled and left whole	1 tablespoon tomato paste
	2 bay leaves
	1 cinnamon stick
1 chicken, approximately 4 pounds, cut into 6 pieces	1/2 teaspoon whole cloves
	1/2 teaspoon whole allspice berries, crushed
All-purpose flour for dredging	
Salt	1/2 teaspoon dried oregano
Freshly ground black pepper	1 1/4 cups red wine
3 cloves garlic, peeled and finely chopped	
8 Roma tomatoes, peeled	

Heat the olive oil in a large skillet and sauté the shallots over medium heat until softened. Remove with a slotted spoon and set aside. Roll the chicken pieces in flour seasoned with salt and pepper, and sauté until browned. Remove with a slotted spoon and set aside. Add the garlic, tomatoes, tomato paste, bay leaves, cinnamon, cloves, allspice berries, oregano, salt and pepper and sauté for 10 minutes. Stir in the wine and cook for another 5 minutes. Add the chicken pieces and shallots back into the saucepan. Stir the mixture and bring to a boil. Then, simmer over low heat for 1 hour or until the sauce thickens and the chicken is tender. Serve with bread. [SERVES 4–6]

CHICKEN BAKED IN YOGURT
WITH SPINACH

GUINEA FOWL "KRASSATO"

Red wine is frequently used to pot-roast game birds, rabbit or hare "Krassato" style (krassi is the Greek word for wine). In this recipe, the guinea fowl are first marinated in lemon juice, herbs and seasoning before roasting with the red wine.

- 2 guinea fowl, approximately 13 ounces each
- Juice of 2 lemons
- 2 tablespoons roughly chopped fresh parsley stalks
- 1 teaspoon dried oregano
- 4 bay leaves
- 2 garlic cloves, peeled and chopped
- 1 teaspoon whole black peppercorns
- Salt
- Freshly ground black pepper
- 4 tomatoes, quartered
- 3 celery stalks, strings removed and roughly chopped
- 1 cup red wine

Marinate the guinea fowl with the lemon juice, parsley stalks, oregano, bay leaves, garlic, peppercorns, salt and pepper in a large bowl in the refrigerator for at least 1 hour. Preheat the oven to 350°F. Place the guinea fowl in a roasting pan. Add the tomatoes and celery and pour the marinade ingredients and red wine into the roasting pan. Bake for 1 1/2 hours or until tender. Baste the guinea fowl from time to time with the liquid in the roasting pan. Carve the guinea fowl and serve with the tomatoes, celery and sauce. Good with mashed potatoes. [SERVES 4–6]

KOTOPOULO PSITO ME GEMISTA KE KRITHARAKI / ROAST CHICKEN WITH STUFFING, ORZO AND GARLIC

In Greece, every household has a tapsi (a round metal roasting pan) that can also be used for a variety of other culinary purposes. Although dishes such as pastitsio, moussaka or stuffed vegetables are commonly cooked in a tapsi, it is also used as a receptacle for drying pulses or fruits in the sun on rooftops. It is always a familiar sight at bakeries in the early morning to see Greeks bringing their dishes to be slow-roasted after the day's bread has been baked. Kritharaki (orzo) or potatoes are always added around the roast to soak up all the juices.

- 1 chicken, about 4 pounds
- 1 tablespoon dried oregano
- Salt
- Freshly ground black pepper
- 1 head garlic, cloves left whole with skins on
- 3 tablespoons olive oil
- Juice of 1 1/2 lemons
- 1 cup water
- 1 pound orzo

FOR THE STUFFING:

- 4 slices white bread, crusts removed
- 4 green onions, including green stems, finely chopped
- 2 tablespoons finely chopped fresh flat-leaf parsley
- 2 tablespoons finely chopped fresh dill
- 2 tablespoons finely chopped fresh mint
- 1/2 teaspoon dried oregano
- 1 tablespoon olive oil
- Juice of 1 lemon
- Salt
- Freshly ground black pepper

TO MAKE THE STUFFING: soak the bread in water for 10 to 15 minutes, then squeeze out all the excess moisture. Crumble the bread into a large bowl. Add all the other ingredients, mix well, season with salt and pepper, and set aside until ready to use.

TO PREPARE THE ORZO: bring a large saucepan of salted water to a boil. Add the orzo and simmer for 10 minutes. Drain in a colander and set aside until ready to use.

TO ROAST THE CHICKEN: preheat the oven to 350°F. Place the stuffing in the chicken cavity. Put the chicken in a large roasting pan (preferably round). Rub the chicken with the oregano, salt and pepper and scatter the garlic cloves around the pan. Drizzle the chicken with the olive oil and add half the lemon juice and water into the roasting pan. Bake for 1 1/2 hours or until tender. Baste the chicken from time to time with the liquid in the roasting pan. During the last 30 minutes of cooking, remove the pan from the oven and add the orzo around the chicken. Drizzle with the remaining lemon juice and water, return to the oven and continue baking for the remaining 30 minutes. Remove from the oven and allow to cool for 10 minutes before serving. Carve the chicken and serve the orzo and garlic directly from the roasting pan. [SERVES 4–6]

LEFT: GUINEA FOWL "KRASSATO"
RIGHT: KOTOPOULO PSITO ME GEMISTA KE KRITHARAKI / ROAST CHICKEN WITH STUFFING, ORZO AND GARLIC

KOTOPOULO KAPAMA
SPICY CHICKEN WITH FRIED POTATOES

Delicious "Kapama" style one-pot dishes are a staple of Greek village meals. They're a chance to slow-cook chicken, lamb or veal, enhanced with a spicy tomato sauce, until the meat almost falls off the bone.

FOR THE CHICKEN:
- 2 tablespoons olive oil
- 4 chicken breasts
- 1 medium-sized yellow onion, peeled and finely chopped
- 5 Roma tomatoes, peeled, seeded and finely chopped
- 1 tablespoon tomato paste
- 1 cinnamon stick
- 1 teaspoon allspice berries
- 1 teaspoon whole cloves
- 2 bay leaves
- 1/2 teaspoon dried oregano
- Salt and black pepper
- 1 cup white wine

FOR THE POTATOES:
- Oil for frying
- 1 pound potatoes, peeled, cut into thin wedges

Heat the olive oil in a large saucepan and sauté the chicken breasts over medium heat until browned. Remove with a slotted spoon and set aside. Sauté the onion in the saucepan until softened, then add the tomatoes and tomato paste and sauté for another 10 minutes. Add the chicken breasts, cinnamon, allspice berries, cloves, bay leaves, oregano, salt, pepper and wine. Stir well and bring the mixture to a boil. Simmer for 1 hour or until the sauce thickens and the chicken is tender.

TO COOK THE POTATOES: heat 2 inches of oil in a deep pan until hot. Carefully drop handfuls of potatoes into the hot oil. Do not overcrowd the pan. Fry until golden. Drain on paper towels. [SERVES 4]

PARTRIDGE "SALMI" WITH RICE

In certain mountainous areas of northern Greece, where game is plentiful, they often cook pheasant, venison, partridge or woodcock using the classic French "Salmis" method — slowly simmering the game with wine, vegetables and aromatics. In this lighter, equally delicious, modern adaptation, I take perdika (partridge) and add a few more vegetables and herbs for a recipe somewhere between a "Salmis" and "Escabeche" style of cooking.

- 2 tablespoons olive oil
- 4 partridges, each cut in half
- 1 teaspoon dried oregano
- Salt
- Freshly ground black pepper
- 6 shallots or baby onions, peeled and left whole
- 2 sticks celery, strings removed and roughly chopped
- 2 bay leaves
- 3 tablespoons roughly chopped fresh parsley with stems
- 1 teaspoon dried oregano
- 1 teaspoon whole black peppercorns
- 1/2 teaspoon whole coriander seeds
- 1 cup white wine

Heat the olive oil in a large saucepan and sauté the partridges, seasoned with the oregano, salt and pepper, over medium heat until browned. Add all the other ingredients, stir the mixture and bring to a boil. Then, simmer for

45 minutes, stirring occasionally, or until the partridges are tender. Serve hot with plain rice or cold with a green salad. [SERVES 4–6]

ORTIKIA SE KLIMATOFILA ME PLIGOURI
ROASTED QUAIL IN VINE LEAVES WITH
BULGUR WHEAT PILAF

In Greece, quail are almost always sprinkled with dried herbs and simply broiled or roasted. Often, they are also wrapped in vine leaves, which prevent them from drying out and give an added depth of flavor.

- 6 vine leaves
- 6 quail
- 6 baby onions, peeled and left whole
- 6 wooden skewers, soaked in water
- Zest of 1 lemon
- 1 tablespoon fresh marjoram
- Salt
- Freshly ground black pepper
- 4 tablespoons olive oil
- 1 1/3 cups bulgur wheat, washed
- 3 pale green banana chiles, seeded and cut in strips
- 3 leeks, washed and chopped

TO PREPARE THE VINE LEAVES: if using fresh leaves, blanch each leaf for a few seconds in a saucepan of boiling water, refresh under cold water and drain on a tea towel. If using pickled leaves, place them in a colander, drain off any excess brine, rinse well under warm water and drain on a tea towel.

TO ROAST THE QUAIL: preheat the oven to 350°F. Stuff each quail cavity with an onion. Wrap each quail with a vine leaf. Secure the vine leaf to each quail by sticking the wooden skewer through the carcass. Place the quail in a roasting pan. Sprinkle with the lemon zest, marjoram, salt, pepper and 2 tablespoons of the olive oil. Bake for 30 to 40 minutes or until tender.

TO COOK THE BULGUR WHEAT PILAF: place the bulgur wheat in a saucepan. Cover with water and bring to the boil. Add the green banana chiles, leeks, remaining 2 tablespoons olive oil and some salt and pepper, and simmer for 15 minutes or until the bulgur wheat has absorbed most of the water. Cover the saucepan with a tea towel until ready to serve.

TO SERVE: remove the quail from the oven and serve on individual plates with some of the pilaf. [SERVES 6]

PREVIOUS PAGES (LEFT):
KOTOPOULO KAPAMA /
SPICY CHICKEN WITH FRIED POTATOES
(RIGHT): PARTRIDGE "SALMI" WITH RICE
RIGHT: ORTIKIA SE KLIMATOFILA ME PLIGOURI /
ROASTED QUAIL IN VINE LEAVES WITH
BULGUR WHEAT PILAF

MEAT

APART FROM THE GREAT RELIGIOUS OR FESTIVE OCCASIONS SUCH AS EASTER, MEAT EATING HAS ALWAYS BEEN A FRUGAL AFFAIR IN GREECE.

In some of the most delicious meat recipes, such as *arni fricassee* (lamb and lettuce stew) or *hirino me selino* (pork and celery stew), the meat plays an almost secondary role to the concentrated flavors of vegetables and *avgolemono* (egg and lemon) sauce. Sadly in the past twenty-five years, to the detriment of the purity of the Mediterranean diet in Greece, increased wealth has seen meat consumption rise to become among the highest in Europe.

Globally, Greek restaurants with their predictable *souvlaki*, *souvlas* and *gyro* dishes have not helped reveal some of the more unusual meat recipes that exist. Veal, pork, lamb and goat are frequently combined with wine, herbs and seasonal vegetables such as artichokes, peas, frisée, zucchini and eggplant in aromatic one-pot stews or oven casseroles. Effortless to make, such dishes always taste better the next day when reheated.

Easter is always celebrated with the *paschal* lamb. After the long religious service on Holy Saturday, *mayeritsa* — an intense soup made from the lamb's intestines, heart, lungs and liver stewed with chopped green onions, celery, dill and avgolemono sauce — breaks the Lenten fast. The real ceremony begins on Easter Sunday when lambs are spit- or oven-roasted and served with simple salads and roast potatoes. Such a feast remains unchanged from ancient times.

KATSIKAKI STO FOURNO / ROAST KID WITH LEMON POTATOES (PAGE 92)

STUFFED LAMB LOIN WITH EGGPLANT

This is a great dish for the barbecue. It can also be cooked in the oven or pan-fried.

FOR THE STUFFING:

- 8 ounces feta, crumbled
- 1 bunch fresh spinach, washed, trimmed and cooked
- $1/4$ cup currants, softened in warm water
- $1/4$ cup pine nuts
- Freshly ground black pepper
- 2 tablespoons olive oil

FOR THE LAMB:

- 1 boned lamb loin (about 1 pound), trimmed and butterflied
- Olive oil
- 6–8 Japanese eggplants, sliced in half
- Salt

TO PREPARE THE STUFFING: mix all the ingredients in a bowl and set aside.

TO COOK THE LAMB: lay the opened lamb loin on a flat surface, place the stuffing down the middle and roll the lamb into a log shape. Tie the loin firmly at regular intervals with kitchen string. Grill the lamb over medium-hot coals for about 20 minutes, turning once and basting with a little olive oil. Sprinkle the eggplant halves with salt, brush with olive oil and barbecue until tender. [SERVES 4]

ARNI ME ANGINARES / LAMB AND ARTICHOKE STEW

Lamb and artichokes are a magical combination that captures all the real flavors and techniques of Greek cooking. This recipe uses seasonal vegetables as the main ingredient, with meat playing a secondary role, to produce a rich and simple stew. Add fresh peas for even more complexity.

- 3 tablespoons olive oil
- 2 medium-sized yellow onions, roughly chopped
- 2 pounds lamb shoulder, cut into large cubes
- 3 tomatoes, peeled and roughly chopped
- $1 1/2$ tablespoons tomato paste
- $2/3$ cup white wine
- 4 fresh artichoke hearts, cut into quarters
- 2 tablespoons finely chopped fresh dill
- 1 tablespoon finely chopped fresh flat-leaf parsley
- Juice of 1 lemon
- Salt
- Freshly ground black pepper

Heat the olive oil in a large casserole dish or saucepan and sauté the onions over medium heat until softened. Add the lamb, stirring constantly until browned. Reduce the heat and add the tomatoes, tomato paste, white wine and enough water to just cover the meat. Simmer, covered, for 30 minutes. Add the artichokes, adding a little more water to just cover if necessary, and simmer until they are tender, about 15 minutes. Add the dill, parsley and lemon juice, and season with salt and pepper to taste. Simmer for another 30 minutes or until the meat is tender and the sauce has reduced. [SERVES 4–6]

LAMB LAGOTO / LAMB, TOMATO, GARLIC AND LEMON STEW

This easy-to-prepare Greek stew hails from the Ionian islands, where it is commonly made with rabbit or lamb. When combined with fresh tomatoes, garlic and lemon juice, it has an intense and quintessential Mediterranean flavor.

- 1 head of garlic, left whole and unpeeled
- 3 tablespoons olive oil
- 3 pounds boned leg of lamb, trimmed and cubed
- $1 1/2$ pounds ripe tomatoes, skinned and roughly chopped
- 1 tablespoon tomato purée
- Salt
- Freshly ground black pepper
- Juice of $1 1/2$ lemons

Place the garlic head in a saucepan of boiling water. Simmer for 15 to 20 minutes or until softened. Meanwhile, heat the olive oil in a large saucepan and sauté the lamb pieces on all sides for about 5 minutes or until browned. Stir in the tomatoes and tomato purée.

Remove the garlic from the water and squeeze each clove into the stew. Season with salt and pepper. Add water just to cover and simmer for $1 1/2$ hours or until tender. During the last 15 minutes of cooking, stir in the lemon juice. Serve with fried or sautéed potatoes and green beans. [SERVES 4–6]

KATSIKAKI OR ARNI STO FOURNO / ROAST KID OR LAMB WITH LEMON POTATOES

In Greece, no special celebration is complete without a whole spit-roasted kid or lamb. The Easter fast is always broken with a feast of roast lamb, potatoes and green salad. For city dwellers unable to spit-roast outdoors, a tapsi (round roasting pan) is used in the oven instead. The free-range goat in Greece is delicious, more delicate in flavor than that available in the West.

- 3–4 pound leg of kid or lamb
- 2 lemons
- Salt
- Freshly ground black pepper
- 1 tablespoon dried oregano
- 4 pounds potatoes, peeled and quartered
- $2/3$ whole head garlic, unpeeled
- 4 tablespoons olive oil
- 1 cup water

Preheat the oven to 350°F. Place the kid or lamb in a large roasting pan. Rub with half a lemon and sprinkle with salt, pepper and the oregano. Place the potatoes and garlic around the meat and salt them lightly. Drizzle the olive oil over the meat and potatoes.

Combine the juice of the remaining lemons with the water and pour over the potatoes. Roast for 2 to $2 1/2$ hours or until the meat is tender. To serve, allow to rest for 10 minutes, then carve onto plates and serve with the potatoes, garlic cloves and some of the roasting juices as gravy. [SERVES 6]

LAMB LAGOTO / LAMB, TOMATO, GARLIC
AND LEMON STEW

ARNI STO HARTI
LAMB BAKED IN PARCHMENT PAPER

Lamb, beef and veal are often baked with vegetables in parchment paper. The tradition comes from the Kleftes, the Greek brigands hiding from the Turks in the mountains and hills who give their name to "Kleftiko" lamb.

3 pounds boned lamb, cut into large 3-inch cubes	Parchment paper and string
1 medium-sized russet potato, peeled and sliced	1/2 tablespoon dried oregano Salt
4 green onions, including stems, quartered	Freshly ground black pepper 1/3 cup white wine
2 cups shelled fresh peas	1 tablespoon olive oil
3 tomatoes, chopped	5 ounces kasseri, kefalotiri or alternative hard cheese, cut into 6 slices

Preheat the oven to 350°F. Combine the lamb, potato, green onions, peas and tomatoes in a large bowl. Cut 6-by-12-inch square pieces of parchment paper. Divide the ingredients from the bowl between the 6 pieces of paper, making sure that they are in the center of each square. Sprinkle with the oregano and seasonings. Drizzle with the white wine and olive oil and place a slice of cheese on top.

Gather the sides up into a purse-like shape, twist the top and secure each parcel with string. Place the parcels on a lightly oiled baking tray and fill the tray with a little water. Bake for 1 1/2 hours. Put each parcel on a plate, cut the strings and serve immediately. [SERVES 6]

RACK OF LAMB STUFFED WITH FETA
AND MINT

This roast makes for a stylish and effortless dinner party presentation. It goes well with beets and skordalia (see page 152) as an accompaniment.

2 racks lamb	1 teaspoon dried oregano
3/4 pound feta, cut into strips	2 tablespoons olive oil
3 tablespoons fresh mint leaves	Salt Freshly ground black pepper

To prepare the lamb, make a slit lengthwise through the back of the racks. Push pieces of feta, coated on either side with mint leaves, into this opening. Tie firmly with string to hold the stuffing in. Alternatively, make a slit lengthwise through the center of each rack and push through the feta and mint stuffing. Rub the meat with dried oregano.

Preheat the oven to 400°F. Heat the oil over a high heat in a large frying pan and sauté the racks briefly until browned. Place the racks in an ovenproof dish and sprinkle with the oregano, salt and pepper. Bake for 15 to 20 minutes. Set aside for 10 minutes in a warm place to rest. Carve into individual portions and serve with beets and skordalia. [SERVES 6]

ARNI "FRICASSEE" / LAMB AND LETTUCE
STEW WITH AVGOLEMONO SAUCE

This is one of my favorite Greek stews. The unusual combination of lamb with romaine lettuce, andithia (frisée) or wild greens is commonplace in Greek homes.

3 tablespoons olive oil	1 small bunch fresh dill, finely chopped
3 pounds boned leg of lamb, trimmed and cubed	Salt
2 bunches green onions, finely chopped	Freshly ground black pepper
2 heads romaine lettuce, washed and finely shredded	FOR THE AVGOLEMONO SAUCE: 2 eggs, lightly beaten Juice of 1 1/2 lemons

Heat the oil in a large saucepan and sauté the lamb for 10 minutes or until browned. Add the green onions, lettuce and dill, and cook for 10 more minutes, stirring constantly until the lettuce wilts. Season with salt and pepper to taste. Add water to just cover the stew and simmer gently for 1 to 1 1/2 hours or until the meat is tender. Allow the stew to cool slightly.

Whisk together the eggs and lemon juice and ladle some of the broth from the stew into the mixture while whisking. Pour the mixture into the stew and stir well with a wooden spoon. Continue to stir over low heat for a few minutes until the sauce begins to thicken. Serve immediately with bread. [SERVES 4–6]

LAMB FILETS WITH ZUCCHINI, POTATO
AND CAPERS

By increasing the recipe amounts, this simple "stir-fry" becomes a great party dish containing some typical Greek ingredients.

2 tablespoons olive oil	2 pounds lamb tenderloin, trimmed and sliced
5 medium-sized potatoes, peeled, parboiled for 10 minutes, sliced	Salt Freshly ground black pepper
4 zucchini, trimmed and sliced lengthways	1/3 cup capers, rinsed 2 tablespoons red wine vinegar

Heat the olive oil in a large frying pan over medium heat and cook the potatoes and zucchini for 5 minutes, turning each slice once. Add the lamb, season with salt and pepper, and sauté for 5 to 7 minutes or until still slightly pink in the center. Add the capers and vinegar and cook over high heat, stirring the mixture, for a few more minutes. Serve immediately with bread to mop up the juices. [SERVES 4–6]

PREVIOUS PAGES: (LEFT) ARNI "FRICASSEE" / LAMB AND LETTUCE STEW WITH AVGOLEMONO SAUCE (RIGHT) ARNI STO HARTI / LAMB BAKED IN PARCHMENT PAPER RIGHT: LAMB FILETS WITH ZUCCHINI, POTATO AND CAPERS

SOFRITO / BRAISED VEAL WITH GARLIC, PARSLEY AND VINEGAR

Another famous dish from Corfu and the Ionian islands. Its Venetian origins are again betrayed in its use of vinegar, garlic and parsley as the main flavorings. This dish can also be simmered on the stovetop for the same cooking time indicated below.

1 1/2 pound veal top round, cut in 1/2-inch slices	4 cloves garlic, peeled and thinly sliced
All-purpose flour, seasoned with salt and black pepper, for dredging	3 tablespoons finely chopped fresh flat-leaf parsley
3 tablespoons olive oil	Salt
	Freshly ground black pepper
	1/2 cup red wine vinegar

Preheat the oven to 375°F. Pound each slice of veal with the flat side of a mallet. Dust both sides of the veal slices with the seasoned flour. Heat the olive oil in a frying pan and sauté the veal slices on both sides until browned. Transfer the slices to a casserole dish in layers, sprinkling each layer with the garlic and parsley. Season with salt and pepper and pour the vinegar over the mixture. Bring the mixture to a boil, then add enough water to just cover the mixture and bring to a boil again.

Cover and bake for 1 1/4 hours or until the veal is tender and the sauce has thickened. Serve with mashed potatoes. (SERVES 4)

MOSCHARI ME MELITZANES VEAL AND EGGPLANT STEW

Meat and eggplant combinations are very popular in Greece. This simple veal stew with added red pepper and chiles makes a delicious midweek meal.

3 tablespoons olive oil	2 pound veal top round, cut into 2-inch cubes
1 pound eggplant, roughly chopped	4 Roma tomatoes, roughly chopped
1 large yellow onion, peeled and roughly chopped	1 teaspoon dried oregano
2 garlic cloves, peeled and finely diced	2 bay leaves
1 red bell pepper, seeded and roughly chopped	1 tablespoon finely chopped fresh flat-leaf parsley
1 red chile, seeded	Salt
	Freshly ground black pepper

Heat the olive oil in a large saucepan and sauté the eggplant pieces for 5 minutes over medium heat until softened. Remove with a slotted spoon and set aside. Repeat the process with the onion, garlic, pepper and chile, then remove with a slotted spoon and set aside. Sauté the veal pieces until browned in the saucepan. Return the eggplant, onion, pepper and chile to the saucepan and stir well. Add the tomatoes, oregano, bay leaves, parsley,

seasonings and enough water to just cover the stew. Bring to a boil and then simmer for 1 1/2 hours or until the veal is tender and the sauce has thickened. Serve with plain rice or potatoes. [SERVES 4]

PASTITSADA POT-ROASTED VEAL WITH PASTA

This famous dish is from Corfu and the Ionian islands. It is popular in tavernas throughout mainland Greece. Sometimes the meat is also cut into thick slices or cubes before pot-roasting. It is always served with pasta, an indication of its Venetian origins. This dish can also be simmered on the stovetop for the same cooking time indicated below.

3 pound veal top round, left whole	2 bay leaves
2 garlic cloves, peeled and thinly sliced	1 cinnamon stick
4 cloves	1/2 cup red wine
2 tablespoons olive oil	1 tablespoon wine vinegar
1 large yellow onion, peeled and finely chopped	Salt
4 Roma tomatoes, coarsely chopped	Freshly ground black pepper
1 tablespoon tomato paste	TO SERVE:
	1 pound macaroni, rigatoni or alternative pasta, boiled
	Grated kefalotiri or parmesan cheese

Preheat the oven to 350°F. Make small cuts in the veal with a sharp knife. Stud the garlic slices and cloves into these cuts. Heat the olive oil in a large casserole dish and sauté the veal on all sides for about 5 minutes or until browned. Remove and set aside. Add the onion and sauté for 5 minutes over medium heat until softened. Stir in the tomatoes, tomato paste, bay leaves and cinnamon and sauté for another 5 minutes. Add the wine and vinegar, season with salt and pepper, stir well and bring to a boil.

Return the veal to the casserole dish. Cover and bake for 1 1/2 to 2 hours or until the veal is tender and the sauce has thickened.

To serve, place the cooked macaroni on a platter. Place the veal on top. Spoon the sauce over the pasta and sprinkle with grated cheese. Carve the veal into slices at the table. [SERVES 4–6]

RIGHT: SOFRITO / BRAISED VEAL WITH GARLIC, PARSLEY AND VINEGAR
FOLLOWING PAGES: (LEFT) PASTITSADA / POT-ROASTED VEAL WITH PASTA
(RIGHT) MOSCHARI ME MELITZANES / VEAL AND EGGPLANT STEW

KOUNELI STIFADO / RABBIT STEW

Rabbit, hare or beef are combined with baby onions, vinegar and spices in this classic one-pot stew. Rabbit or hare are best marinated overnight, although the dish works equally well with a short marinating time.

1 rabbit, cut into 6 pieces	2 garlic cloves, peeled
4 tablespoons olive oil	and finely sliced
3 pounds baby onions or	2 bay leaves
shallots, peeled whole	1 cinnamon stick
1 tablespoon tomato paste	3 whole cloves
FOR THE MARINADE:	1 teaspoon dried oregano
1/2 cup red wine	1 teaspoon allspice berries
4 tablespoons red wine	Salt
vinegar	Freshly ground black pepper

Place the rabbit pieces in a large non-reactive bowl. Add the marinade ingredients, cover and refrigerate for at least 6 hours, preferably overnight.

Heat the olive oil in a large saucepan and sauté the onions for 5 minutes over medium heat until softened. Remove with a slotted spoon and set aside. Sauté the rabbit pieces until browned in the saucepan. Return the onions to the saucepan, add the marinade mixture, tomato paste and enough water to just cover the stew. Bring to a boil and then simmer for 1 1/2 to 2 hours or until the rabbit is tender and the sauce has thickened. [SERVES 4–6]

HIRINO SELINO AVGOLEMONO / PORK WITH CELERY AND AVGOLEMONO SAUCE

Celery or celeriac (also known as celery root) is a favorite combination with pork. If using celeriac, cut into large cubes and parboil before adding to the stew.

3 tablespoons olive oil	1 teaspoon dried oregano
3 pounds boned leg of pork,	Salt
trimmed and cubed	Freshly ground black pepper
1 medium-sized yellow onion,	FOR THE AVGOLEMONO SAUCE:
peeled and sliced	2 eggs, lightly beaten
1 bunch celery, including	Juice of 1 1/2 lemons
leaves, trimmed and sliced	
(or 1 1/2 to 2 pounds celeriac)	

Heat the oil in a large saucepan and sauté the pork for 10 minutes or until browned. Add the onion, celery and oregano, and cook for a further 10 minutes, stirring constantly until the celery begins to soften. Add water to just cover the stew, season to taste with salt and pepper, and simmer gently for 1 hour or until the meat is tender. Allow the stew to cool slightly.

Whisk together the eggs and lemon juice and ladle some of the broth from the stew into the mixture while whisking. Pour the mixture into the stew and stir well with a wooden spoon. Continue to stir over a low heat for a few minutes until the sauce begins to thicken. Serve immediately with bread. (SERVES 4)

MOSCHARI GIOUVETSI ME KRITHARAKI BAKED BEEF WITH ORZO

Giouvetsi is the name for a type of earthenware dish used to make meat stews with pasta that are baked in the oven. Some of the best dishes come from the island of Sifnos and Lesbos and can be found in kitchen stores throughout Greece.

4 tablespoons olive oil	1 sprig fresh thyme
2 pounds stew beef, cut into	1 teaspoon dried oregano
3-inch chunks	1 tablespoons tomato paste
1 medium-sized yellow onion,	1/2 cup red wine
peeled and finely chopped	Salt
4 large tomatoes,	Freshly ground black pepper
peeled and chopped	1 pound orzo
4 cloves garlic, peeled	1/3 cup grated kefalotiri or
and diced	parmesan cheese

Preheat the oven to 350°F. Heat the olive oil in a large frying pan and sauté the beef until browned. Add the onion, tomatoes, garlic, thyme and oregano and cook for 10 minutes, stirring occasionally. Add the tomato paste, red wine and enough water to cover the mixture. Season to taste with salt and pepper. Transfer the mixture to a large earthenware or ovenproof casserole dish and bake for 1 to 1 1/2 hours.

Meanwhile, parboil the orzo for 10 minutes in a large saucepan until almost soft but not quite fully cooked. Drain in a colander and place around the beef mixture during the last 20 minutes of cooking. The orzo will absorb all the liquid in the pot. To serve, sprinkle the cheese on top and serve with a green salad. [SERVES 4]

KOUNELI STIFADO / RABBIT STEW

SPETSOFAI / SAUSAGE AND PEPPER STEW

This dish is served in all the tavernas of villages nestled around Mount Pelion, above the town of Volos in Thessaly. Its fame has spread throughout Greece where it is served usually as a meze. Substitute Italian sausage or chorizo if necessary.

- 3 tablespoons olive oil
- 3 pounds spicy pork sausages, sliced into thick pieces
- 2 pounds mixed red and green bell peppers, seeds and membranes removed, cut into strips
- 1 medium-sized yellow onion, peeled and roughly chopped
- 3 large tomatoes, peeled and roughly chopped
- 3 cloves garlic, peeled and finely diced
- 1 tablespoon tomato paste
- 1 cup red wine
- 1 teaspoon dried oregano
- Salt
- Freshly ground black pepper

Heat the olive oil in a large frying pan over medium heat and sauté the sausages for 10 minutes, or until browned. Remove from the pan. Add the peppers and onion to the same pan and sauté for 10 minutes, or until softened. Add the tomatoes, garlic, tomato paste, red wine and oregano, season with salt and pepper, and stir the mixture well. Simmer over low heat for 20 minutes, then stir the sausages back into the stew.

Simmer for another 20 minutes or until the sauce thickens. If necessary, add a little water during the cooking process. Serve with boiled rice or bread. [SERVES 6]

HIRINO ME PRASSA / PORK AND LEEK STEW

In winter, pork is also combined with leeks. This simple stew makes a perfect midweek meal served with plainly boiled rice.

- 3 tablespoons olive oil
- 3 pounds boned picnic shoulder of pork, trimmed and cubed
- 6 leeks, trimmed and sliced
- 1 medium-sized yellow onion, peeled and chopped
- 1 teaspoon dried oregano
- Salt
- Freshly ground black pepper

Heat the oil in a large saucepan and sauté the pork for 10 minutes or until browned. Add the leeks, onion, oregano, salt and pepper and cook for another 10 minutes, stirring constantly until the leeks begin to soften. Add water to just cover the stew and simmer gently for 1 hour or until the meat is tender and the sauce has thickened. Allow the stew to cool slightly. Serve with rice or bread. [SERVES 4–6]

LEFT: SPETSOFAI / SAUSAGE AND PEPPER STEW
ABOVE: SOUTZOUKAKIA SMIRNEIKA / SMYRNA-STYLE RISSOLES

SOUTZOUKAKIA SMIRNEIKA SMYRNA-STYLE RISSOLES

This is a famous "Greek" dish from Smyrna (modern day Izmir, Turkey), brought to the mainland in 1922 when over 500,000 Greeks in Asia Minor were forced to flee their homes. Today, it can be found in most tavernas as a regular menu item. The meatballs can be either fried or baked in the oven and are always simmered in a tomato sauce.

- 2 slices white bread, crusts removed
- 1 pound ground beef
- 1 medium-sized yellow onion, peeled and grated
- 3 cloves garlic, peeled and finely diced
- 1 tablespoon finely chopped fresh flat-leaf parsley
- 1 egg, beaten
- 2 teaspoons ground cumin
- Salt
- Freshly ground black pepper
- All-purpose flour for dredging
- Olive oil for frying
- 1 cup tomato sauce (see page 152)

Soak the bread in water for 10 to 15 minutes, then squeeze out all the excess moisture. Combine the bread, ground beef, onion, garlic, parsley, egg, cumin and seasonings in a large bowl. Shape into oval meatballs about 2 inches long and roll in flour. Preheat the oven to 350°F. Heat the olive oil in a large frying pan and sauté the meatballs on all sides for about 10 minutes over medium heat. Remove with a slotted spoon and place in a baking dish. Cover with the tomato sauce and bake for 20 to 25 minutes. Serve with boiled rice. [SERVES 4 / MAKES ABOUT 20 RISSOLES]

HIRINO GEMISTO / STUFFED PORK LOIN

Pork loin is often simply stuffed with vegetables, garlic and a few dried herbs. On islands ruled by the Venetians, such as the Ionian and Cycladic group, recipes like this one still survive, with a more Italian influence.

1 boneless loin of pork, 5 pounds in weight

1 red bell pepper, seeded and roughly chopped

1 small red onion, peeled and sliced

1 medium-sized carrot, peeled and sliced

2 hard-boiled eggs, peeled and quartered

1 garlic clove, peeled and finely diced

1 tablespoon roughly chopped fresh flat-leaf parsley

1 teaspoon dried oregano

Salt

Freshly ground black pepper

FOR THE SALAD:

1 bunch arugula

2 tomatoes, quartered

FOR THE DRESSING:

Olive oil

Red wine vinegar

Salt

Freshly ground black pepper

Preheat the oven to 450°F. With a sharp knife, prepare the pork loin by making a long open slit in the middle of the meat without separating it completely. Lay it open flat. Combine the bell pepper, onion, carrot, eggs, garlic, parsley and oregano in a bowl. Season the meat with salt and pepper, then spread the stuffing in the center. Roll the meat into a log shape and tie the loin firmly at regular intervals with kitchen string.

Place in a roasting pan, sprinkle the skin with a little salt and roast for 15 minutes and then at 350°F for 1 1/2 hours, taking the meat out when the juices run clear when pierced with a thin skewer.

TO SERVE: after the pork has rested, carve into slices and serve with the salad, dressed with a little olive oil, vinegar and seasonings. [SERVES 6]

LAMB "KLEFTIKO" WITH LEMON POTATOES

Although this recipe hardly ever appears in mainland Greece, it has become one of the most famous Greek dishes, thanks to the pioneering efforts of the Cypriot and Greek restaurateurs around the world. It takes its name from the Klefts who cooked lamb in lidded pots buried in charcoal and earth so that no tell-tale wafts of smoke or aromas would give their positions away. This is a delicious way to slow-cook lamb until it is almost falling off the bone.

FOR THE LAMB:

2 shoulders of lamb about 4 pounds in weight total, each shoulder cut into 3 chunks

4 pounds potatoes, peeled and quartered

1 head of garlic, unpeeled and cut in half across the middle

2 teaspoons dried oregano

3 bay leaves

1 teaspoon fresh marjoram

Salt

Freshly ground black pepper

3 tablespoons olive oil

Juice of 2 lemons

1/2 cup water

Preheat the oven to 325°F. Combine the meat, potatoes and garlic in a large earthenware or ovenproof casserole dish. Sprinkle with the herbs, seasonings, olive oil, lemon juice and water. Seal the dish firmly with kitchen foil or cover with a lid and bake for 3 hours or until the meat is falling off the bone. Check from time to time to see if the meat or potatoes need any more liquids, and turn down the oven to a lower heat if necessary. Serve with green salad and bread. [SERVES 6–8]

PIKTI / JELLIED HAM

This modern interpretation of a classic dish is certainly easier to make than the traditional Greek recipe using a pig's head and trotters. I have added oranges in homage to a traditional sausage combination of pork and oranges used in the Mani in the Peloponnese. It makes for a refreshing light summer lunch or supper dish.

1 pound unsmoked ham

1 yellow onion, peeled and left whole

4 cloves

1 celery stick, halved

1 carrot, peeled and sliced

2 bay leaves

2 cloves garlic, peeled

1/2 teaspoon allspice berries

1/2 teaspoon black peppercorns

1 1/2 tablespoons finely chopped fresh flat-leaf parsley

2 oranges, peeled and cut into segments

FOR THE JELLY:

Scant 4 1/2 teaspoons (1 1/2 packets) unflavoured powdered gelatin, softened in 1/4 cup of water for 5 minutes

4 tablespoons white wine vinegar

Juice of 2 oranges

Salt

Freshly ground black pepper

Place the ham, onion studded with the cloves, celery, carrot, bay leaves, garlic, allspice berries and peppercorns in a large saucepan and cover with water. Bring to a boil, skimming any foam from the surface. Lower the heat and simmer for 45 minutes. Strain the stock through a cheesecloth-lined sieve into a large bowl, discarding all the vegetables and aromatics. Transfer the ham to a plate and set aside to cool. Cut the ham into rough strips and place in a large bowl. Add the parsley and orange segments and combine.

TO ASSEMBLE THE JELLY: add the gelatin to the heated stock mixture in the bowl and stir until the gelatin dissolves. Add the vinegar and orange juice and season the liquid with salt and pepper. Pour the jellied stock over the ham and refrigerate until set. To serve, scoop out of the bowl onto plates and serve with bread and green salad. [SERVES 6]

FISH + SHELLFISH

MOST GREEKS HAVE A NATURAL AFFINITY WITH THE SEA. DESPITE BEING SADLY OVER-FISHED, THE AEGEAN SEA IS STILL HOME TO OVER 250 EDIBLE FISH VARIETIES, AND THE GREEKS ARE PASSIONATE ABOUT ALL OF THEM.

Although most seafood is simply grilled, boiled or fried, there are numerous recipes that call for more complex ingredients and cooking methods. Two popular styles of cooking fish are *savoro*, where the fish is fried with vinegar and rosemary, and *marinato*, where small fish are fried in flour then placed in earthenware pots and covered with a tomato sauce and vinegar. These two methods were rife around the Mediterranean in the days before refrigeration as a method of preserving fish. The Ottoman occupation has left a love of stuffing or baking fish and *midia* (mussels) with pine nuts, raisins, tomatoes, onions and parsley.

The seasons also play an important role in the Greek fish diet. During *Sarokosti*, the 40 fasting days of Lent, crustacea such as *garides* (prawns) and *karavides* (langoustines) are consumed in large quantities. On *Kathari Deftera* (Clean Monday), before Easter, only bloodless shellfish such as clams, oysters, cockles and limpets are eaten. In summer and especially in August, *kolios* (mackerel) are at their best and are fried or baked "Plaki" style (with tomatoes, onions and herbs). September is the month when everybody fishes for large *thrapsala* (flying squid) or *kinigos* (mahi mahi) as they begin to migrate down from the Black Sea. During the winter months, hearty dishes of *bakaliaros me skordalia* (salt cod battered and fried with garlic sauce) and grilled or stewed *heli* (eels) are eaten.

Some of the most exciting recipes are for octopus, squid and cuttlefish. All are slowly stewed or baked with unusual combinations of rice, macaroni, onions, spinach, eggplant, potatoes, aromatics and wine. These stark, simple marriages of earth and sea also seem to embody the colorful, strange juxtapositions at the heart of much seasonal Aegean cooking. Octopus are also the favorite mezes in every backstreet ouzerie or waterfront taverna, where they are hung out to dry in the sun on broomsticks or pieces of wire. Blackened to an almost sticky toffee consistency, the sensual barbecued coil of tentacles remains the quintessential proletarian taste of the Aegean Sea.

RED MULLET

BAKALIAROS ME PRASSORIZO
COD WITH LEEK RICE

The sweetness of the leeks and onions goes well with the richness of the pan-fried cod in this simple dish, ideal for a winter meal.

FOR THE LEEK RICE:
- 3 tablespoons olive oil
- 3 cups washed and thickly sliced leeks
- 1 medium-sized white onion, peeled and sliced
- 1 3/4 cups long-grain white rice
- 1 tablespoon finely chopped fresh dill
- 1 teaspoon dried mint
- Salt
- Freshly ground black pepper

FOR THE FISH:
- 2 pounds cod or whiting fillets, cut into chunks
- Salt
- Freshly ground black pepper
- 2 tablespoons olive oil
- 3 green onion bulbs, peeled and roughly chopped
- 2 lemons, halved

TO MAKE THE LEEK RICE: heat the olive oil in a large saucepan over medium heat, and sauté the leeks and onion for about 5 minutes or until softened. Add the rice, dill, mint, salt and pepper and sauté for a further 5 minutes. Add enough water to just cover the ingredients and stir well. Simmer for 15 to 20 minutes or until the rice is cooked and most of the liquid has been absorbed, stirring occasionally to prevent the mixture from sticking. At the end, if the mixture is too liquid, remove the saucepan from the heat, stretch a thick tea towel over the pan and replace the lid (the cloth will absorb any extra moisture). Set aside for a few minutes.

TO PREPARE THE FISH: season the fish fillets with salt and pepper. Heat the olive oil in a large skillet over medium heat, and cook the green onions and fish fillets for about 10 to 15 minutes or until the fish and onions are cooked.

TO SERVE: place the leek rice in individual bowls and top with the fish fillets and green onions. Serve with a squeeze of lemon. [SERVES 6]

SARDELLES STO FOURNO
BAKED SARDINES WITH GREEN PEPPER

This easy-to-prepare dish is equally good hot or cold.

- 1 pound fresh sardines, washed, cleaned and butterflied
- 2 cloves garlic, peeled and finely chopped
- 1 green bell pepper, seeded and cut into strips
- 1 tablespoon finely chopped fresh marjoram
- 1 tablespoon finely chopped fresh flat-leaf parsley
- Salt
- Freshly ground black pepper
- 2 tablespoons olive oil

Preheat the oven to 350°F. Layer the sardines in a shallow baking dish, sprinkling the garlic, pepper strips, marjoram, parsley and seasonings between the layers. Drizzle with the olive oil and bake for 20 minutes. Serve hot or cold. [SERVES 4]

GAVROS DIPLOTIGANIA / "DOUBLE-FRIED" STUFFED ANCHOVIES

When fresh anchovies and sardines are plentiful, all manner of inventive dishes are turned out. This Spanish tortilla-style anchovy dish is good for a light lunch.

- 1 1/2 pounds fresh anchovies, washed, cleaned and butterflied
- 3/4 cup all-purpose flour
- 2 medium-sized yellow onions, grated
- 6 tablespoons breadcrumbs
- 6 tablespoons finely chopped fresh flat-leaf parsley
- 3 cloves garlic, peeled and finely chopped
- Salt
- Freshly ground black pepper
- 2 tablespoons olive oil

Roll the anchovies in the flour and lay them out, butterflied. Mix the onions, breadcrumbs, parsley and garlic together and season to taste with the salt and pepper. Heat the olive oil in a large cast-iron skillet over a low heat. Place a layer of anchovies, skin-side down, fanned around the pan.

Sprinkle the stuffing mixture over the anchovies and press down lightly with a spatula. Layer the rest of the anchovies, skin-side up, over the stuffing and fanned around the pan. When the bottom layer of anchovies is cooked after about 5 minutes, place a large plate over the skillet and invert the skillet carefully. Slide the uncooked layer back into the pan. Alternatively, use a spatula to turn the anchovies. Cook for another 5 minutes and serve while still warm. [SERVES 6]

KOLIOS PLAKI
BAKED MACKEREL "PLAKI" STYLE

Mahi mahi, bonito and cod are other good fish to use in this classic recipe. Whatever fish are used, if they are small they can be left whole or filleted if preferred. Tomatoes, potatoes and peppers are sometimes added to the vegetable medley.

- 1 1/2 pounds whole mackerel, cleaned and cut into chunks
- 4 large carrots, peeled and thinly sliced
- 2 medium-sized yellow onions, peeled and finely chopped
- 3 cloves garlic, peeled and finely chopped
- 3 bay leaves
- Salt
- Freshly ground black pepper
- 3 tablespoons olive oil
- 4 tablespoons finely chopped fresh flat-leaf parsley
- 2/3 cup white wine
- Juice of 1 lemon

Preheat the oven to 350°F. Put the fish, carrots, onions, garlic and bay leaves into a baking dish. Season with salt and pepper and sprinkle the olive oil and parsley over the mixture. Add the white wine, lemon juice and a little water. Bake for 30 minutes or until the fish and vegetables are cooked and the sauce has thickened. Serve hot or cold. [SERVES 4–6]

BAKALIAROS ME PRASSORIZO /
COD WITH LEEK RICE

KAKAVIA / FISH SOUP

Ever since the time of the ancient Greeks, fishermen have been making this soup with leftover fish from their catch. Said to be the humble predecessor of bouillabaisse, it almost certainly travelled to Marseilles when the ancient Greeks colonized the south of France. Optional extras may include tomatoes, lemon zest, saffron, stale bread and rice.

6 shallots or baby onions, peeled and halved (alternatively use 2 medium-sized onions, peeled and sliced)	1 stalk celery with the tops, sliced and chopped
4 large potatoes, peeled and roughly chopped	3 tablespoons finely chopped fresh flat-leaf parsley
3 carrots, peeled and sliced	2 pound selection of firm fish like scorpion fish, rock cod, snapper, monkfish, mullet, bream
1 zucchini, trimmed and roughly chopped	Salt
	Freshly ground black pepper
	Juice of 1 1/2 lemons

Place the vegetables and parsley in a large saucepan. Cover with water and boil over medium heat for 10 minutes. Meanwhile, clean and gut the fish. If small leave whole, otherwise cut into fillets. Place the fish carefully on top of the vegetables, reduce the heat and cook for another 10 to 15 minutes until the fish and vegetables are cooked. Carefully remove the fish and vegetables and set aside. Strain the stock and return it to the pot. Debone the fish and remove the heads. Return the deboned fish and the vegetables back into the strained stock, and season with salt and pepper. Bring back to a boil, then simmer for 5 to 10 minutes. Place fish and vegetables in soup bowls and pour the broth over. Squeeze lemon juice into each bowl and serve with toasted bread. [SERVES 4]

TONOS STIFADO / TUNA STEW

Tuna responds equally well to the classic "Stifado" style of cooking meat. This is a great winter dish.

2 pounds fresh tuna, cut into large chunks	4–6 bay leaves
Juice of 1 lemon	2 tablespoons tomato paste
1 tablespoon salt	8 Roma tomatoes, finely chopped
6 tablespoons olive oil	Salt
4 pounds baby onions, peeled whole	Freshly ground black pepper
3 cloves garlic, peeled and finely chopped	2 sticks cinnamon
1 large yellow onion, peeled and thinly sliced	6 whole cloves
	3 tablespoons whole allspice, crushed with a mortar and pestle
	2 1/2 cups red wine

PSARI VRASTO / BOILED SNAPPER AND BREAM WITH VEGETABLES

TO PREPARE THE TUNA: bleach the tuna steaks by putting them in a bowl with the lemon juice and salt. Add enough water to just cover. Cover with plastic wrap and refrigerate for 30 minutes to 1 hour.

TO PREPARE THE STEW: heat one-third of the olive oil in a large saucepan over medium heat and brown the whole onions for 5 minutes, stirring occasionally. Transfer the onions to a bowl. Heat another third of olive oil in the same saucepan, add the garlic, sliced onion and bay leaves, and soften over medium heat for 5 minutes, stirring constantly. Stir in the tomato paste, tomatoes and salt and pepper to taste, and simmer for 15 minutes. Add the browned whole onions, cinnamon, cloves, allspice and red wine, stir and continue to cook over low heat for about 8 minutes, while you cook the tuna.

TO COOK THE TUNA: heat the remaining 2 tablespoons olive oil in a large skillet and sear the tuna for about 4 minutes each side. Transfer the tuna to the sauce, mix in well and continue to simmer for 20 to 30 minutes or until the sauce has thickened. To serve, spoon the stew into warmed bowls and serve with mashed potatoes, plain rice or bread. [SERVES 6–8]

PSARI VRASTO / BOILED SNAPPER AND BREAM WITH VEGETABLES

In Greece, whole fish such as snapper and bream are poached with vegetables and aromatics. The fish and vegetables are then removed to a platter. The remaining fish stock is usually turned into psarosoupa avgolemono *(fish and avgolemono soup) and served before the fish.*

1 yellow onion, peeled and sliced	**FOR THE VEGETABLES:**
1 stick celery, halved	10 shallots or baby onions, peeled and left whole
1 small bunch parsley, including stalks	15 small Yukon gold potatoes, peeled and left whole
1 lemon, sliced	4 stalks celery, trimmed and chopped into 4-inch strips
2 bay leaves	3 zucchini, trimmed and thickly sliced
1 tablespoon fresh thyme	4 carrots, peeled and chopped
1/2 tablespoon black peppercorns	6 baby leeks, trimmed and cut in half
Salt	**TO SERVE:**
3 tablespoons olive oil	1/2 cup ladolemono sauce (see page 153)
4 pounds small snapper and bream	

Fill a large saucepan or fish poacher with water and bring to a boil. Add the sliced onion, celery, parsley, lemon, bay leaves, thyme, peppercorns, salt and olive oil. Cover and simmer for 10 minutes. Carefully lower the fish into the pan, cover and simmer for 15 to 20 minutes or until the fish is cooked. Meanwhile, fill another large saucepan with salted water and bring to a boil. Add all the vegetables and simmer for 15 to 20 minutes until cooked.

To serve, carefully lift the fish and lemon slices out of the saucepan and place on a platter. Remove the vegetables from the other saucepan and drain in a colander. Place in bowls or on the platter with the fish. Serve immediately with ladolemono sauce. [SERVES 6]

WHITEBAIT "MARINATO"

In Greece, atherina (sand smelt), gavros (anchovies), marida (picarel) and gopa (bogue) are the favored small fish for frying. They are lightly floured, fried until crisp and served with a squeeze of lemon. They are also treated in this classic style for preserving fish: marinating it in emulsified vinegar, wine and herbs. Whitebait respond equally well to this treatment.

2 pounds whitebait, washed	1/2 teaspoon dried oregano
Juice of 2 lemons	Salt
1/2 cup white wine vinegar	1/2 teaspoon black peppercorns
1/2 cup white wine	All-purpose flour for dredging
1 teaspoon coriander seeds	Olive oil for frying

Marinate the whitebait with the lemon juice in a bowl. Cover and refrigerate for at least 15 minutes or until ready to use. In a small saucepan, bring the vinegar, wine, coriander seeds, oregano, salt and peppercorns to a boil and then simmer for 15 minutes. Meanwhile, lightly flour the whitebait. Heat some olive oil in a large skillet, add the floured whitebait and cook for about 3 to 5 minutes until golden brown.

Drain the whitebait on paper towels and transfer to a serving bowl. Pour over the hot marinade and serve hot or cold. [SERVES 6]

BAKALIAROS ME SKORDALIA / COD WITH SKORDALIA

Skordalia is traditionally served with bakaliaros (salt cod) or galeos (dog shark) but goes equally well with other firm-fleshed fish. This recipe can also be made with swordfish, marlin, bonito or tuna.

1 3/4 pounds cod or whiting, skin and bones removed, cut in cubes	grated
	3 tablespoons breadcrumbs
	Salt
1 tablespoon whole allspice, crushed	Freshly ground black pepper
2 teaspoon cinnamon	1 1/2 tablespoons olive oil
1 tablespoon sesame seeds	Skordalia [see page 152]
Zest of 1 lemon, finely	

Mix the cod, spices, sesame seeds, lemon zest, breadcrumbs and seasonings in a bowl. Heat the olive oil in a large skillet and cook the mixture for 10 to 15 minutes, stirring frequently, or until golden brown. Transfer to a platter and serve with the skordalia and a green salad. [SERVES 4–6]

PAN-FRIED SQUID WITH ONIONS AND LEMON JUICE

When fresh from the nets, squid is usually put straight into the pan. In this recipe, I have combined it with onions, lemon juice and a little white wine for a more substantial dish.

2 tablespoons olive oil	1 cup white wine
2 white onions, peeled and thinly sliced	Juice of 1 1/2 lemons
	Salt
1 1/2 pounds squid, cleaned, body and tentacles separated and cut into pieces	Freshly ground black pepper
	Lemon or lime wedges

Heat the oil in a large skillet and sauté the onions for 5 minutes or until softened. Add the squid pieces and cook, stirring, over medium heat for 5 minutes. Add the wine and lemon juice and cook for another 3 minutes. Transfer the onion and squid mixture to a platter. Increase the heat to high and cook the pan juices for a few minutes to reduce slightly. Pour the juices over the squid and season with salt and pepper. Serve with extra wedges of lemon or lime and crusty bread to mop up the juices. [SERVES 4–6]

ABOVE: WHITEBAIT "MARINATO"
RIGHT: PAN-FRIED SQUID WITH ONIONS
AND LEMON JUICE

ASTAKOS ME DOMATES
BAKED LOBSTER WITH TOMATOES

Various species of the spiny lobster (Palinurus vulgaris) *are commonly found in Greece. They are mostly served simply boiled with ladolemono sauce. I like this colorful dish with a rich tomato sauce baked in the oven.*

2 lobsters, approximately 3 to 4 pounds in total weight	2 cups tomato sauce (see page 152)
	1/2 tablespoon finely chopped fresh flat-leaf parsley

Bring a large saucepan of salted water to a boil. Place the lobsters in the saucepan and simmer, covered, for 15 to 20 minutes. Then remove the lobster from the water and drain.

Meanwhile, place the tomato sauce in a saucepan and simmer for 10 minutes. Preheat the oven to 350°F.

Cut the lobsters in half lengthwise and clean by removing the sand sac, gills and stomach. Place the halves in a large ovenproof baking dish. Pour the tomato sauce over the lobsters and bake for 10 minutes. Serve immediately with parsley sprinkled on top. [SERVES 4]

PALAMIDA ME MARATHO
GRILLED BONITO WITH FENNEL

Palamida (bonito) *is a wonderful fish when just caught. Try it baked "Plaki" style, grilled or fried with herbs. In Greece, it is also salted and preserved in olive oil. It makes a delicious meze with ouzo.*

1 1/2 pounds bonito or snapper fillets	FOR THE MARINADE:
	Zest of 1/2 lemon
1 tablespoon olive oil	1 clove garlic, peeled and diced
8 ounces baby fennel bulbs and stalks, trimmed	1 teaspoon oregano
1 cup white wine	1 tablespoon finely chopped fresh dill
Juice of 2 lemons	Salt
Zest of 1 lemon	Freshly ground black pepper
Salt	2 tablespoons olive oil
Freshly ground black pepper	

Combine the marinade ingredients in a bowl with the fish fillets. Cover and refrigerate for at least 30 minutes.

Heat the olive oil in a large skillet and sauté the fennel for 5 minutes until softened. Add the white wine, lemon juice and zest, salt and pepper and simmer, stirring occasionally, for 10 minutes or until the fennel is tender and the sauce has thickened.

Cook the fish fillets on an oiled cast-iron grill over medium heat, for about 5 to 7 minutes each side, depending on the thickness of the fillets, or until cooked. Baste with the remaining marinade ingredients while cooking.

To serve, transfer the fennel to a platter, place the fish fillets on top, spoon any remaining sauce from the pan over the fish fillets and serve immediately. [SERVES 4]

SARDELLES MARINATES ME KREMMIDIA
MARINATED SARDINES WITH ONION SALAD

Fresh anchovies, garfish or sardines can all be used in this recipe. It makes a great dinner party starter.

FOR THE SARDINES:	2 tablespoons coriander seeds, roughly crushed with a mortar and pestle
2 pounds sardines, scaled, washed, cleaned and butterflied	
	Salt
3 tablespoons salt	Freshly ground black pepper
Red wine vinegar	TO SERVE:
FOR THE ONION SALAD:	Olive oil for drizzling
5 white onions, peeled and thinly sliced	2 tablespoons capers, rinsed
	2 tablespoons finely chopped fresh flat-leaf parsley
6 tablespoons olive oil	Red wine vinegar (optional)

In a large, deep glass bowl, place the butterflied sardines in layers, sprinkling a little salt on each layer. Add enough red wine vinegar to just cover the layers, then cover with a weighted plate and refrigerate for 48 hours.

TO PREPARE THE ONION SALAD: mix the onions, olive oil and crushed coriander seeds in a bowl. Season to taste with salt and pepper. Cover and set aside for 30 minutes.

TO SERVE: drain the sardine fillets, slice lengthways into fillets, and put on individual plates. Drizzle with olive oil and sprinkle with the capers, parsley and additional red wine vinegar, if desired. Serve with the onion salad. [SERVES 6–8]

LEFT: ASTAKOS ME DOMATES /
BAKED LOBSTER WITH TOMATOES
ABOVE: PALAMIDA ME MARATHO /
GRILLED BONITO WITH FENNEL

MIDIA KRASSATA
MUSSELS WITH RED WINE SAUCE

Mussels are farmed in many coastal areas of Greece. They are often cooked this way or baked "Saganaki" style with tomatoes and feta.

2 tablespoons olive oil	2 pounds mussels, washed and beards removed
1 yellow onion, peeled and finely chopped	1 cup red wine
2 bay leaves	Salt
4 sprigs fresh thyme	Freshly ground black pepper

Heat the olive oil in a large skillet and sauté the onion, bay leaves and thyme for 5 minutes until softened. Add the mussels and wine, cover and simmer for about 10 minutes or until all the mussels have opened. Transfer the mussels to a serving bowl and keep warm. Bring the wine to the boil over a high heat, stirring, for about 5 minutes or until the sauce thickens. Season to taste with salt and pepper. Pour over the mussels and serve. [SERVES 4]

GARIDES SAGANAKI
BAKED PRAWNS WITH TOMATOES AND FETA

This classic dish of baked prawns is found in the fish tavernas of Athens, especially around Piraeus and Tourkalimano.

2 tablespoons olive oil	Salt
1 yellow onion, peeled and finely chopped	Freshly ground black pepper
2 garlic cloves, peeled and diced	8 large raw prawns, cleaned and deveined with tail shells left intact
4 tomatoes, peeled and roughly chopped	6 ounces feta
1 teaspoon tomato paste	1 tablespoon finely chopped fresh flat-leaf parsley

Preheat the oven to 400°F. Heat the olive oil in a large ovenproof skillet. Add the onion and garlic and sauté for 5 minutes or until softened. Add the tomatoes and tomato paste and cook over medium heat for 10 minutes. Season to taste with salt and pepper. Add the prawns and cook for 5 minutes more. Scatter the feta on top and bake for 10 minutes. Sprinkle with the parsley and serve. [SERVES 4]

LEATHERJACKETS SAVORO-STYLE

A similar fish (and member of the trigger fish family) is found in Greece under the name of gouronopsaro *(pig fish). Substitute flounder, sole or any kind of flat fish in this popular recipe for frying fish.*

6 leatherjackets, each 250 g, heads removed, gutted and skinned	freshly ground black pepper
3 tablespoons butter	6 small sprigs of fresh rosemary, washed and roughly chopped
3 tablespoons olive oil	3 tablespoons red wine vinegar
salt	

Select a frying pan large enough to accommodate two fish at a time. Heat 1 tablespoon of butter and 1 tablespoon of olive oil in the pan. Season the fish with salt and pepper and then fry two at a time in the pan with a third of the rosemary for 8 to 10 minutes on each side, adding 1 tablespoon of red wine vinegar at the end of cooking.

Transfer the fish and pan juices to an ovenproof serving dish in a warm oven and repeat the process until all the fish have been cooked. To serve transfer to warmed plates, spooning the pan juices over the fish and accompany the fish with a green salad. [SERVES 6]

SOUPIES ME SPANAKI /
CUTTLEFISH AND SPINACH STEW

This is a wonderful dish with complex flavours. It is so rich that it needs little accompaniment except some bread to mop up the sauce.

4 tablespoons olive oil	750 g spinach, washed and chopped
1 large brown onion, peeled and finely sliced	2 tablespoons finely chopped fresh flat-leaf parsley
750 g cuttlefish, washed, cleaned and chopped	1 tablespoon tomato paste
5 tomatoes, peeled and roughly chopped	175 ml white wine
	salt
	freshly ground black pepper

Heat the oil in a large saucepan and sauté the onion for 5 minutes or until softened. Add the cuttlefish pieces and cook, stirring, over a medium heat for 5 minutes. Add the tomatoes, spinach and parsley and cook, stirring, for another 5 minutes until the spinach begins to wilt. Add the tomato paste, wine and enough water to just cover the mixture, then season to taste with salt and pepper. Stir well and simmer over a low heat for 1 hour or until the cuttlefish is tender and the sauce has thickened. Serve with bread.
[SERVES 4–6]

LEFT: (TOP) MIDIA KRASSATA /
MUSSELS WITH RED WINE SAUCE
(BELOW) GARIDES SAGANAKI /
BAKED PRAWNS WITH TOMATOES AND FETA
FOLLOWING PAGES: (LEFT) LEATHERJACKETS
"SAVORO" STYLE
(RIGHT) SOUPIES ME SPANAKI /
CUTTLEFISH AND SPINACH STEW

MAYATICO ME SKORDALIA
KINGFISH WITH SKORDALIA

Kingfish (drum or croaker) is an excellent fish to pan-fry or grill, especially when served with some pungent skordalia and a simple green salad.

- 2 pounds kingfish fillets or firm white-fleshed fish
- 1 tablespoon roughly chopped fresh oregano
- 1 tablespoon roughly chopped fresh mint
- Salt
- Freshly ground black pepper
- 3 tablespoons olive oil
- Juice of ¹/₂ lemon
- Skordalia (see page 152)

Place the fish, oregano, mint, salt and pepper and half the olive oil in a bowl. Cover and refrigerate for at least 30 minutes or until ready to use. Heat the remaining 1¹/₂ tablespoons olive oil in a large saucepan and cook the fillets with the marinade ingredients for about 5 to 7 minutes on each side.

Add the lemon juice to the pan for the last few minutes of cooking. Transfer the fish onto plates, pouring any pan juices over the fish, and serve with a spoonful of skordalia and a green salad. [SERVES 4]

BARBOUNIA STO FOURNO ME AMBELOFILA
RED MULLET BAKED IN VINE LEAVES WITH
VEGETABLES

Since the time of the ancient Greeks, red mullet, one of the most prized Mediterranean fish, have been wrapped in vine leaves to be grilled or fried, baked or roasted in the embers of a dying fire.

- 4 medium-sized red mullet or red snapper, each about ¹/₂ pound in weight, cleaned and left whole
- 4 large fresh vine leaves, washed and blanched
- 1 pound potatoes, peeled and roughly chopped
- 1 pound zucchini, trimmed and roughly chopped
- 1 pound tomatoes, roughly chopped
- 2 cloves garlic, peeled and diced
- 1 teaspoon dried oregano
- Salt
- Freshly ground black pepper
- 2 tablespoons olive oil
- ¹/₂ cup water

Wrap the fish in the vine leaves. Cover and refrigerate until ready to use. Preheat the oven to 350°F. Place the potatoes, zucchini, tomatoes and garlic in an ovenproof dish. Sprinkle with the oregano, salt and pepper. Drizzle with the olive oil and water. Bake for 20 minutes.

Remove the fish from the refrigerator. Take the dish out of the oven and place the fish on top of the vegetables. Replace in the oven and bake for 25 to 30 minutes or until the fish are cooked. Serve immediately. [SERVES 4]

LEFT: MAYATICO ME SKORDALIA /
KINGFISH WITH SKORDALIA
ABOVE: BARBOUNIA STO FOURNO ME AMBELOFILA /
RED MULLET BAKED IN VINE LEAVES WITH VEGETABLES

BOURDETTO / SPICY FISH STEW

This colorful fish stew comes from the Ionian islands. I also add Spanish paprika for an added intensity of flavor and heat. Use any kind of firm-fleshed fish fillets.

- 2 tablespoons olive oil
- 2 medium-sized yellow onions, peeled and sliced
- ¹/₂ cup white wine
- ¹/₂ cup water
- 2 tablespoons tomato paste
- 1 teaspoon cayenne
- ¹/₂ teaspoon paprika
- Salt
- 2 pounds grey mullet fillets, or alternative fish fillets such as halibut
- 2 tablespoons finely chopped fresh flat-leaf parsley

Heat the olive oil in a large skillet and sauté the onions for 5 minutes until softened. Add the wine, water, tomato paste, cayenne and paprika. Sauté, stirring, for a further 10 minutes, then season to taste with salt. Carefully add the fish fillets, adding a little more water if necessary to just cover the fish, and simmer for 20 to 25 minutes or until the fish is tender and the sauce has thickened. Serve the fish, onions and sauce on a platter. Sprinkle with the parsley, if desired, and serve with plain rice or potatoes. [SERVES 6]

XIPHIAS ME VLITA / SPICED SWORDFISH FILLETS WITH AMARANTH

This recipe is inspired by the commonplace usage of herbs and spices, such as those listed below, in ancient Greece. Today, such usage has sadly diminished and would seem too adventurous for most modern Greeks.

1 teaspoon fennel seeds	1 1/2 pounds swordfish fillets,
1 teaspoon cumin seeds	cut into 8 pieces
1 teaspoon aniseed	Olive oil for frying
1 teaspoon caraway seeds	**TO SERVE:**
1/2 teaspoon paprika	2 bunches (2 pounds) amaranth
All-purpose flour for dredging	or spinach, trimmed, cooked
Salt	in water, drained and dressed
Freshly ground black pepper	with olive oil and lemon juice

Using a mortar and pestle, crush the fennel, cumin, aniseed, caraway seeds and paprika. Sprinkle into a large shallow bowl. Add some flour, salt and pepper. Dip the fish fillets into the spice mixture and leave for a few minutes to marinade. Heat a little olive oil in a large skillet and, when hot, add the fish fillets.

Cook for about 5 to 7 minutes on each side, depending on the thickness of the fillets, until the fish is golden brown. To serve, divide the amaranth between serving plates and top with the fish fillets. [**SERVES 4**]

XIPHIAS MARINATOS / SWORDFISH MARINATED WITH TOMATOES

This easy-to-prepare recipe makes an ideal light summer lunch or supper.

4 swordfish steaks,	2 bay leaves
approximately 1 pound in	2–3 tablespoons white wine
weight total	vinegar
3 cloves garlic, peeled,	Salt
crushed and roughly	Freshly ground black pepper
chopped	2 tablespoons olive oil
3 tomatoes, peeled and diced	All-purpose flour for dredging

Marinate the swordfish steaks with the garlic, tomatoes, bay leaves, vinegar, salt and pepper. Cover and refrigerate for at least 30 minutes. Heat the olive oil in a skillet. Remove the swordfish from the marinade.

Dip each side of the swordfish steaks in the flour and sauté in the skillet for about 3 to 4 minutes on each side. Remove to a warm plate.

Add all the marinade ingredients to the skillet, turn up the heat and sauté for a few minutes or until the sauce thickens. Pour this sauce over the swordfish steaks and serve immediately with a watercress and onion salad. [**SERVES 4**]

LEFT: XIPHIAS ME VLITA / SPICED
SWORDFISH FILLETS WITH AMARANTH
ABOVE: BOURDETTO / SPICY FISH STEW
(PAGE 123)

OCTAPODI KRASSATO / OCTOPUS STEWED WITH RED WINE AND ONIONS

Sometimes I think that the Greeks have as many recipes for octopus as the Portuguese have for salt cod. This rich stew is just one of the inventive combinations. Others recipes combine octopus with rice or pasta, green olives and fennel, or eggplants and potatoes.

1 large octopus (6 to 8	2 cloves garlic, peeled and
pounds) or 2 medium-sized	finely chopped
octopuses (3 to 4 pounds each)	3 bay leaves
1 tablespoon red wine vinegar	1 1/2 cups red wine
4 tablespoons olive oil	Salt
2 pounds shallots or baby	Freshly ground black pepper
onions, peeled whole	2 tablespoons finely chopped
1 tablespoon tomato paste	fresh flat-leaf parsley

Clean the octopus by removing its beak, turning its head inside out and discarding the ink sac and other organs. Rinse the octopus well and place in a large, heavy pot with the red wine vinegar. Cook over high heat for about 5 to 10 minutes, stirring occasionally, until the octopus begins to curl and turn a pinkish color. Then lower the heat, cover the pot and let the octopus simmer in the juices that it releases, stirring occasionally, for 1 hour or until beginning to become tender. Add a small amount of water if there is no liquid in the pot. Allow the octopus to cool, drain and cut into thick slices.

Heat the olive oil in a large saucepan and sauté the onions, stirring, over medium heat for 5 minutes or until softened. Reduce the heat and simmer for a further 10 minutes, shaking the pan occasionally to prevent the onions from sticking. Add the octopus pieces, tomato paste, garlic, bay leaves and wine to just cover the mixture. Bring to a boil over medium heat and cook, stirring constantly, for 5 minutes. Reduce the heat and simmer for 30 minutes or until the octopus is tender and the sauce has thickened. Season with salt and pepper and sprinkle with the parsley. Serve warm with some bread to mop up the juices. [**SERVES 6**]

TO MAKE THE SAUCE: heat the olive oil in a large skillet and sauté the onion for 5 minutes until softened. Add the other ingredients and simmer, stirring, for 20 minutes.

TO PREPARE THE SQUID: preheat the oven to 325°F. Use a teaspoon to stuff the squid sacs with the rice mixture, being careful not to overfill them. Seal the openings with small wooden or metal skewers. Place the stuffed squid in a large ovenproof baking dish. Add the reserved tentacles and pour over the tomato sauce. Bake for 1 to 1 1/2 hours or until the squid and rice are tender and the sauce has thickened. Serve hot or cold. [SERVES 6]

BRANDADA ME DOMATES
BRANDADE WITH TOMATOES AND ONIONS

I have only ever eaten brandada *in Santorini and presume that it is a legacy of Venetian and Genoese traders and other occupants on the island. It is not a common dish but my version, with its use of allspice, cinnamon and nutmeg, certainly has some of the flavor of certain classic Greek dishes. The tomatoes and onions can be either fried, grilled or roasted as in this recipe.*

3 pounds potatoes, peeled and quartered	2 pounds cod, bream or similar firm white-fleshed fish fillets
8 allspice berries	6 Roma tomatoes, halved
8 black peppercorns	4 large green onion bulbs, peeled and quartered
2 bay leaves	1/2 tablespoon fresh rosemary
1 cinnamon stick	Salt
A little grated nutmeg	Freshly ground black pepper
6 cups milk	Olive oil for drizzling

Cook the potatoes in plenty of boiling water for 20 minutes, then set aside in the pot. Meanwhile, place all the spices in another saucepan with the milk. Bring slowly to a boil, then add the fish and simmer for 10 to 15 minutes until tender.

Preheat the oven to 400°F. Place the tomatoes and green onions on a baking sheet. Sprinkle with the rosemary, salt and pepper and drizzle with a little olive oil. Bake for about 20 minutes or until cooked.

Strain the fish mixture in a sieve, reserving the milk. Allow the fish fillets to cool slightly, then transfer to a plate and discard the spices. Drain the potatoes and return to a saucepan with the fish. Add the reserved milk and work the mixture into a rough mash. Season and add a little olive oil. Serve immediately with the tomatoes and onions. [SERVES 4–6]

KALAMARAKIA GEMISTA / STUFFED SQUID

This is one of my favorite recipes—well worth the effort of carefully stuffing the squid. The dish is equally delicious served cold.

14 medium-sized squid, approximately 3 pounds in weight, cleaned and tentacles separated from the sacs	1 tablespoon raisins, soaked in warm water for 10 minutes
FOR THE STUFFING:	1 tablespoon dried mint
1 tablespoon olive oil	Salt
1 medium-sized yellow onion, peeled and finely diced	Freshly ground black pepper
1 cup long-grain white rice	FOR THE SAUCE:
2 tablespoons finely chopped fresh flat-leaf parsley	1 tablespoon olive oil
1 1/2 tablespoons pine nuts	1 medium-sized yellow onion, peeled and finely diced
	1/2 cup white wine
	2 cups tomato sauce (see page 152)

TO MAKE THE STUFFING: heat the olive oil in a large skillet and sauté the onion for 5 minutes until softened. Add the rice and sauté, stirring, until golden brown. Add all the other ingredients and a little water and simmer, stirring, for 5 minutes more.

RIGHT: KALAMARAKIA GEMISTA / STUFFED SQUID
ABOVE: BRANDADA ME DOMATES / BRANDADE
WITH TOMATOES AND ONIONS

DESSERTS + DRINKS

IN MOST GREEK HOMES, IT IS COMMON PRACTICE TO OFFER GUESTS SOME-
THING SWEET AS A SIGN OF HOSPITALITY.

Homemade *glika tou koutaliou* (spoon preserves) such as *vissino* (cherries), *sika* (figs), *nerantzi* (Seville orange), *kidoni* (quince) and *karidia* (walnut) or *loukoumia* (Turkish delight) are favorite offerings, normally served with a small cup of Greek coffee and a glass of iced water.

Greeks are fanatical about fresh fruit. At most restaurants and tavernas, a meal always ends with some seasonal fruit: in winter, baked quince, sliced apple sprinkled with cinnamon or a simple bowl of yogurt, walnuts and honey; in summer, a platter of fresh fruit such as melon, watermelon, grapes or peaches usually ends up on the table.

However, there is also a huge repertoire of cakes, pastries and desserts available. Few are made at home these days, with the exception of simple fried batters and classic biscuits such as *loukoumades* (honey balls), *diples* (deep-fried honeyed pastries), *xerotigana* (pastry whorls), *melomakarona* (honeyed bis-cuits) and *kourabiedes* (shortcake). Most are bought at the *zacharoplastia* (pastry shops) that abound. In these shops, other typical sweets such as *baklavas*, *galaktoboureko* (custard pie), *revani* (semolina and almond cake), *rizogalo* (rice pudding) and *moustalevria* (grape must pudding) are commonly sold together with cream-filled cakes, cookies, chocolates and preserves.

GLIKA TOU KOUTALIOU / SPOON PRESERVES

MOUSTALEVRIA / GRAPE MUST DESSERT

A favorite dessert that is always made during the grape harvest with moustos (grape must). This simpler version is also found in pastry shops throughout Greece.

4 tablespoons cornstarch	6 grapes, peeled,
1 tablespoon sugar	halved and seeded
3 1/4 cups grape juice, freshly	TO SERVE:
squeezed and strained	1 1/2 tablespoons sesame seeds
through muslin, or	1 teaspoon cinnamon
ready-made grape juice	

Mix the cornstarch and sugar together in a bowl. Bring the grape juice to a boil in a saucepan. Slowly mix one-quarter of the grape juice with the cornstarch mixture, then stir this back into the remaining juice in the saucepan. Cook over low heat, stirring until the mixture thickens and becomes translucent.

Lightly oil 4 individual molds and divide the peeled grape halves among them. Remove the mixture from the heat and pour into the molds. Set aside to cool and then cover and refrigerate until set. To serve, unmold the desserts onto individual plates and sprinkle with the sesame seeds and cinnamon. [SERVES 4]

GREEK COFFEE

There is an art to making "Greek" or "Turkish" coffee. It is best to make no more than 2 cups at a time so that each person can share some of the prized thick foam that forms on top. Try and use a briki (a long handled brass or metal pot with a pouring lip), watching over it carefully to ensure that the foam does not boil over. To order Greek coffee in a café, simple ask for sketo (unsweetened), metrio (with sugar), gliko (sweet) or vari gliko (very sweet).

3 heaping teaspoons	2 teaspoons sugar
Greek-style coffee	2 small coffee cups of water

Put all the ingredients into a briki or similar small saucepan. Heat over low heat, stirring occasionally, until the mixture begins to rise.

Take off the heat. Immediately return to the heat until the mixture begins to rise again.

Pour a little of the froth slowly into the two coffee cups, then pour the remaining coffee into the cups. Serve with glasses of iced water. [MAKES 2 CUPS]

RIGHT: MOUSTALEVRIA / GRAPE MUST DESSERT
BELOW: SUMMER FRUITS
FOLLOWING PAGES: (LEFT) GREEK COFFEE
(RIGHT) IPOVRIHIO / SUBMARINE (PAGE 134)

VISSINO GLIKO / SOUR-CHERRY PRESERVE

This is one of the most popular spoon sweets. The syrup from this preserve is also used to make vissinada, *a popular sour-cherry cordial served with iced water. Bottles are also available commercially.*

2 pounds sour cherries	Juice of 1 lemon, strained
4 cups granulated sugar	2 1/2 cups water

Wash and stone the cherries in a large bowl so that all the juices are preserved. Place the cherries and their juices, sugar, lemon juice and water in a heavy saucepan. Bring to the boil, skimming off any froth with a slotted spoon, and then simmer for about 10 minutes.

Remove the cherries with a slotted spoon to a bowl, allow to cool slightly and then transfer into sterilized jars. Continue to boil the syrup until the syrup thickens and reaches the setting point, then pour over the cherries in the sterilized jars. Store in a cool place and serve as spoonfuls on small plates with accompanying glasses of iced water. [SERVES 6]

IPOVRIHIO / SUBMARINE

Named after the Greek word for "submarine," this is a popular thirst quencher and sugar-hit combination in Greek cafes. Vanilla fondant is available in Greek and Middle Eastern delicatessens.

4 tablespoons vanilla fondant	4 glasses iced water

Place a long-handled tablespoon of vanilla fondant in each glass of iced water. Suck on the vanilla fondant between sips of water. [SERVES 4]

FASKOMILO / SAGE TEA

Sage grows abundantly in Greece and is collected at the end of the summer. It is never used in cooking but is widely drunk as a soothing medicinal tea to cure colds, sore throats, inflamed gums and upset stomachs.

2 tablespoons dried sage	2 teaspoons honey
2 glasses of water	

Place the sage and water in a small saucepan. Heat over low heat until the mixture begins to come to a boil. Strain into the 2 glasses, add a teaspoon of honey to each and stir well. [SERVES 2]

MELOMAKARONA / HONEYED BISCUITS

Another Christmas and New Year festive favorite in all Greek households, these spicy cookies are also called Phoenikia *after the Phoenicians, who are said to have introduced them into Greece.*

FOR THE SYRUP:
- 6 tablespoons honey
- 1/2 cup sugar
- 1/2 cup water
- 1/2 cup minus 1 tablespoon lemon juice

FOR THE FILLING:
- 1 cup walnuts, finely chopped
- 3 tablespoons unsalted butter
- 1/2 teaspoon cinnamon
- 2 tablespoons of the syrup

FOR THE DOUGH:
- 8 tablespoons unsalted butter
- 2/3 cup olive oil
- 1/3 cup confectioners' sugar
- Juice of 1 orange
- 1/2 teaspoon ground cloves
- 1/4 teaspoon nutmeg
- 1 tablespoon brandy
- 2 1/3 cups all-purpose flour, sifted
- 1 teaspoon baking powder

FOR THE TOPPING:
- 3 tablespoons walnuts, finely chopped
- 1 teaspoon cinnamon

TO MAKE THE SYRUP: place the honey, sugar, water and lemon juice in a saucepan and simmer, stirring, for 10 minutes.

TO MAKE THE FILLING: combine the walnuts, butter, cinnamon and 2 tablespoons of syrup in a bowl.

TO MAKE THE BISCUITS: preheat the oven to 350°F. Beat the butter, oil and confectioners' sugar together in a bowl until light and fluffy. Add the orange juice, cloves, nutmeg and brandy and beat for a few more minutes. Add the flour and baking powder slowly, beating continuously until smooth. Knead the mixture by hand into a smooth dough, adding a little more flour if necessary. Take small pieces of the dough and form into small egg shapes. Flatten each biscuit and place a teaspoon of filling in the center. Carefully work the dough around the filling, pressing the dough to seal it. Place the biscuits on a baking sheet and bake for 20 minutes or until a pale golden color. Transfer to a wire rack and allow to cool.

Dip each biscuit in the syrup with a slotted spoon and transfer to a serving platter. Sprinkle with the walnuts and cinnamon. Allow to cool before serving. [MAKES ABOUT 25 BISCUITS]

RIGHT: VISSINO GLIKO / SOUR-CHERRY PRESERVE
FOLLOWING PAGES: (LEFT) FASKOMILO / SAGE TEA
(RIGHT, TOP) MELOMAKARONA / HONEYED BISCUITS
(RIGHT, BELOW) KOURABIEDES /
CHRISTMAS SHORTCAKE (PAGE 138)

MELITINIA / SWEET CHEESE PASTRIES

These pastries originate in the Cyclades. Soft mizithra goat's milk cheese is used as a filling, but ricotta can be substituted.

2 cups mizithra or ricotta	3 cups all-purpose flour, sifted
2 cups granulated sugar	1/3 cup olive oil
2 eggs, lightly beaten	3 tablespoons water
1/2 teaspoon vanilla extract	

Preheat the oven to 350°F. Place the cheese, sugar, eggs and vanilla in a large bowl. Mix well so that all the ingredients are blended. Add 1 tablespoon of the flour into the mixture. To make the pastry, place the rest of the flour in a large bowl. Add the olive oil and begin to make a dough by kneading the mixture. Gradually add the water, kneading the mixture into a soft dough, adding more water if necessary. Roll out the pastry on a lightly floured board as thinly as possible.

Cut 3 1/2-inch circles in the pastry with a wine glass or pastry cutter. Pinch the sides upward to make octagonal cases. Place the pastries on an oiled baking sheet and spoon a tablespoon of filling into each pastry case. Bake for 30 minutes or until golden brown. [**MAKES ABOUT 24 PASTRIES**]

KOURABIEDES / CHRISTMAS SHORTCAKE

These melt-in-the-mouth shortbread cookies are traditionally served at Christmas and New Year.

1 cup unsalted butter	1 2/3 cups all-purpose flour
1 1/2 cups confectioners' sugar plus extra for dusting	2/3 cup blanched almonds, finely chopped
1 teaspoon vanilla extract	1/2 teaspoon baking powder
1 egg yolk	Pinch salt

Preheat the oven to 350°F. In a bowl, beat the butter and sugar together until light and fluffy. Add the vanilla and egg yolk and beat for a few more minutes. Add the flour, almonds, baking powder and salt and beat for a few more minutes until smooth.

Knead the mixture by hand into a smooth dough. Take walnut-sized pieces of the dough and form into crescent shapes. Place on a baking sheet and bake for 12 to 15 minutes or until pale golden. Transfer to a wire rack and allow to cool. Sift confectioners' sugar over the kourabiedes and store in a cake tin until ready to serve. [**MAKES ABOUT 20**]

REVANI / SEMOLINA AND ALMOND CAKE

This syrupy semolina and almond cake is surprisingly light and easy to make. It is popular throughout Greece and always available in most pastry shops.

2 1/3 cups granulated sugar	2/3 cup all-purpose flour
3 cups cold water	1 cup plus 2 tablespoons fine semolina
1 small stick cinnamon	1 tablespoon baking powder
4 whole cloves	3/4 cup blanched almonds, finely chopped
Zest of 1 orange	1 teaspoon vanilla extract
7 ounces (14 tablespoons) unsalted butter	2 tablespoons brandy
6 eggs	

Combine 1 1/3 cups of the sugar with the cold water in a saucepan and simmer over a low heat until the sugar has dissolved. Then, add the cinnamon stick, cloves and orange zest and simmer for another 15 minutes. Remove the cinnamon stick and cloves and allow to cool.

Preheat the oven to 350°F. Place the butter in a bowl and beat until soft and light with an electric blender or hand whisk. Slowly add the remaining 1 cup sugar, then add the eggs individually, beating thoroughly after each addition. In another bowl, sift the flour, semolina and baking powder together. Add the chopped almonds and mix well. Gradually add this mixture to the batter, beating continuously. Finally, add the vanilla and brandy to the mixture and pour into a buttered 9-by-12-inch rectangular baking pan.

Bake for 30 minutes. Remove from the oven and score the cake into diamond shapes with a sharp knife. Spoon the cooled syrup over the cake and allow to cool. Decorate each portion with a blanched almond. [**MAKES ABOUT 18 PORTIONS**]

RIGHT: MELITINIA / SWEET CHEESE PASTRIES
FOLLOWING PAGES: (LEFT) REVANI / SEMOLINA AND ALMOND CAKE
(RIGHT) HALVAS / SEMOLINA PUDDING (PAGE 142)

GALAKTOBOUREKO / CUSTARD PIES

This classic dessert can be found throughout Greece. Few people make it at home, such is its familiarity as a daily staple that it is widely available in bakeries, pastry shops and snack bars.

1 package commercial filo pastry	1 teaspoon vanilla extract
Melted butter	3 tablespoons unsalted butter, melted
FOR THE CUSTARD:	FOR THE SYRUP:
6 1/4 cups milk	2 cups granulated sugar
6 eggs, lightly beaten	1 cup water
1 cup granulated sugar	2 tablespoons fresh lemon juice
1 cup plus 2 tablespoons fine semolina	Zest of 1/2 lemon
Grated zest of 1/2 lemon	

TO MAKE THE CUSTARD: put the milk in a saucepan. Bring to a boil slowly, then remove from the heat. Beat the eggs and sugar together in a bowl until frothy. Add the semolina, grated lemon zest and milk and blend well.

Place this mixture back into the saucepan and cook over low heat, stirring, for about 10 minutes or until the mixture thickens. Add the vanilla and melted butter, stir well, and continue to simmer for 5 minutes more. Remove from the heat and allow to cool.

TO PREPARE THE PIES: preheat the oven to 350°F. Allow 2 1/2 filo sheets per pie. Lay the 2 filo sheets down on a flat surface. Place the half-sheet over one half of the 2 filo sheets. Fold the other half of the 2 filo sheets over the half-sheet. Brush with the melted butter. Place 3 to 4 tablespoons of the custard filling along the length of the filo at one end and carefully roll the filo and custard filling up in a roll.

Repeat the process with the other pies. Place the pies on a baking sheet, sprinkle with a little water, and bake for 40 minutes or until the pies are golden brown. Leave to cool.

TO MAKE THE SYRUP: place the sugar, water, lemon juice and lemon zest in a saucepan and simmer, stirring, for 10 minutes. To serve, place the pies on a platter and serve either hot or cold with the syrup poured over them or served as a separate sauce. [MAKES 6 PIES]

BAKLAVAS

One of the most famous Greek pastries, baklava is also easy to make and always a success as a dessert.

FOR THE PASTRY:	FOR THE SYRUP:
4 cups walnuts, finely crushed	6 tablespoons honey
1 1/2 cups granulated sugar	1 1/2 cups warm water
2 teaspoons cinnamon	1 tablespoon fresh lemon juice
1 package commercial filo pastry	
Olive oil or melted butter	

TO MAKE THE PASTRY: preheat the oven to 350°F. Combine the walnuts, sugar and cinnamon in a bowl. Oil a 9-by-12-inch rectangular baking pan. Place a sheet of filo pastry in the pan, brush with a little olive oil, and sprinkle some of the walnut mixture on top. Repeat the process until all the sheets of filo and walnut mixture are used up. Bake for 45 minutes or until the top is golden brown. Remove from the oven, allow to cool and score the cake into diamond shapes with a sharp knife.

TO MAKE THE SYRUP: put the honey, water and lemon juice in a saucepan and simmer, stirring, for 10 minutes. Pour over the baklava and allow to cool for several hours before serving. [SERVES 10]

HALVAS / SEMOLINA PUDDING

There are many kinds of halva in Greece. This easy recipe, traditionally made at home, is one of the most famous and popular.

FOR THE SYRUP:	FOR THE HALVA:
3 cups water	1 cup olive oil
2 cups fresh orange juice	2 1/4 cups fine semolina
1 tablespoon fresh lemon juice	1/4 cup sliced almonds, finely chopped
2 cups granulated sugar	1/4 cup pine nuts
1 cinnamon stick	TO SERVE:
1 piece fresh lemon peel	1 teaspoon cinnamon
1/2 tablespoon cloves	

TO MAKE THE SYRUP: place the water, orange juice, lemon juice and sugar in a saucepan and bring to a boil. Add the cinnamon stick, lemon peel and cloves. Simmer over low heat for 10 minutes. Allow to cool, then remove the cinnamon stick, lemon peel and cloves by passing through a fine sieve.

TO MAKE THE HALVA: heat the olive oil in a large saucepan over medium heat. Add the semolina, almonds and pine nuts. Cook the mixture over a low heat, stirring constantly, until the mixture begins to turn a golden color or for about 15 to 20 minutes, being careful not to burn the mixture. Remove from the heat.

Carefully pour the syrup over the semolina mixture, stirring with a wooden spoon. Cover with a kitchen cloth and leave for 10 minutes to let the mixture absorb the syrup. Spoon the mixture into individual bowls and allow to cool. Before serving, sprinkle each bowl with cinnamon. [SERVES 4]

RIGHT: GALAKTOBOUREKO / CUSTARD PIES
FOLLOWING PAGES: (LEFT, FROM FRONT)
DIPLES / DEEP-FRIED PASTRIES DIPPED IN HONEY
XEROTIGANA / PASTRY WHORLS (PAGE 147)
(RIGHT) A TYPICAL END TO A MEAL IS
YOGURT, WALNUTS AND HONEY

DIPLES
DEEP-FRIED PASTRIES DIPPED IN HONEY

These honeyed dough squares are often made in advance and kept in air-tight containers after deep-frying. They can also be made in knot and bow shapes.

5 egg yolks	1/4 teaspoon baking soda
1 egg white	2 cups all-purpose flour
3 tablespoons butter, melted	Vegetable oil for
3 tablespoons granulated	deep-frying
sugar	FOR THE TOPPING:
Grated zest and juice	5 tablespoons honey
of 1 orange	2 tablespoons finely chopped
1 teaspoon vanilla extract	pistachios and walnuts

TO MAKE THE DOUGH: beat the egg yolks and egg white until light and fluffy. Slowly add the butter, sugar, orange zest and vanilla, beating continuously. Sift the baking powder, baking soda and 3/4 cup of the flour together in a bowl and gradually add to the mixture. Add the remaining 1 1/4 cups flour and mix until a soft dough forms. Knead until the dough is elastic and smooth, then divide into three balls. Lightly flour each ball and roll out very thinly, rotating the dough as it is rolled to help stretch it out. Roughly cut into 5-inch squares.

TO MAKE THE DIPLES: heat the oil in a large saucepan suitable for deep-frying. Drop a few pieces of dough at a time into the hot oil and fry for 3 minutes or until golden brown. Drain on paper towels and then cool on racks. Heat the honey and orange juice in a small saucepan.

TO SERVE: place the diples on a large platter or individual plates, spoon the honey over and sprinkle with the nut mixture. [MAKES ABOUT 24]

XEROTIGANA / PASTRY WHORLS

This Cretan speciality can also be found in many pastry shops on the Greek mainland. Just outside Chania, the nuns of Chryssopigi convent make some of the best that I have ever tasted. This recipe, adapted from a recipe by the food writer Nikos Stavroulakis, a Chania inhabitant, makes very similar pastries to those made at the convent.

1 2/3 cups all-purpose flour, sifted	FOR THE SYRUP:
6 tablespoons water	6 tablespoons honey
Juice of 1/2 orange	3 tablespoons water
1 1/2 tablespoon olive oil	2 tablespoons
1/3 cup raki or ouzo	fresh lemon juice
Vegetable oil for deep-frying	

TO MAKE THE PASTRY WHORLS: place the flour in a bowl and slowly add the water, orange juice, olive oil and raki. Mix until well combined, adding a little more water if necessary, and then knead the mixture into a smooth and elastic dough.

Set aside, covered with a cloth, for 1 hour, then knead the dough again. Roll out the pastry on a lightly floured board as thinly as possible. Cut into 4-by-1 1/2-inch strips.

Heat the oil in a large saucepan suitable for deep-frying. Twist a strip of pastry around a fork, then lower it quickly into the hot oil, using a spaghetti twirling motion to make a whorl. After about 3 minutes or when the whorl is a golden color, remove with a slotted spoon and drain on paper towels. Keep warm until all the whorls are cooked.

TO MAKE THE SYRUP: place the honey, water and lemon juice in a saucepan and simmer, stirring, for 10 minutes. Set aside to cool.

TO SERVE: place on a large platter or individual plates and spoon the syrup over the pastry whorls. [MAKES ABOUT 12]

RIZOGALO / RICE PUDDING

This creamy, sweet dish is another favorite Greek pudding, widely available in pastry shops.

4 1/2 cups milk	2 teaspoons cornstarch
1/3 cup long-grain white rice,	2 egg yolks, lightly beaten
washed	1 teaspoon vanilla extract
1 cinnamon stick	1/2 cup granulated sugar
Zest of 1/2 lemon	TO SERVE:
2 tablespoons cold milk	1 teaspoon cinnamon

Place the milk in a saucepan and simmer over low heat for 5 minutes. Add the rice, cinnamon stick and lemon zest, and simmer for 15 minutes or until the rice is tender. In a small saucepan, whisk the cold milk, cornstarch and egg yolks together and simmer over low heat until thickened.

Add this mixture, together with the vanilla and sugar, to the milk and rice mixture. Simmer, stirring, for another 5 minutes. Remove the mixture from the heat. Set aside to cool, remove the cinnamon stick, and pour into 4 individual bowls. Refrigerate until ready to use. Sprinkle each bowl with cinnamon before serving. [SERVES 4]

RIZOGALO / RICE PUDDING

ORANGE AND POMEGRANATE JELLY

Oranges and pomegranate trees grow all over Greece. Although pomegranates are mostly eaten as a fruit, they are sometimes added to savory and sweet dishes. This simple and refreshing jelly is a perfect end to a summer meal.

1 1/2 tablespoons (2 packets) powdered gelatin	1/2 pomegranate, seeds scooped out and pith removed
1/3 cup water	1 orange, peeled and pith removed, segments halved
2 tablespoons granulated sugar	
1 1/4 cups fresh orange juice	TO SERVE:
1 1/4 cups fresh pomegranate juice	1/2 pomegranate, seeds scooped out and pith removed
Vegetable oil	

Stir the gelatin and water together in a saucepan over low heat, until the gelatin has dissolved. Add the sugar, orange juice and pomegranate juice to the gelatin mixture and stir well. Lightly oil six individual molds (or one large 4 1/2 cup mold) with vegetable oil. Put the pomegranate seeds and orange pieces into the molds.

Pour the liquid into the molds, then cover and refrigerate until firmly set. To serve, unmold on individual plates and surround with pomegranate seeds. [SERVES 6]

LOUKOUMADES / HONEY BALLS

These small honey balls are similar to doughnuts and are equally popular as a mid-morning snack in Greek cafes and pastry shops.

1/4 ounce (1 packet) dry yeast	FOR THE SYRUP:
1 cup warm water	6 tablespoons honey
1 2/3 cups all-purpose flour, sifted	3 tablespoons water
	Vegetable oil for deep-frying
1/2 teaspoon salt	1 teaspoon cinnamon

TO MAKE THE BATTER: dissolve the yeast in 1/2 cup of the warm water for 15 minutes or until it becomes frothy. Place the flour and salt in a bowl. Make a well in the center and add the yeast solution and remaining 1/2 cup warm water. Mix well to make a thick batter. Cover with a kitchen towel and leave for 1 hour in a warm place or until the batter has doubled in size.

TO MAKE THE SYRUP: place the honey and water in a saucepan and simmer, stirring, for 10 minutes. Set aside to cool.

TO MAKE THE HONEY BALLS: heat the oil in a large saucepan suitable for deep-frying. Drop heaping tablespoons of the batter into the hot oil, turning them as they puff up. Fry for about 3 minutes or until they are golden brown. Drain on paper towels and keep warm until all the batter is used. To serve, place on a large platter or individual plates, spoon the syrup over and sprinkle with cinnamon. [MAKES ABOUT 26]

SIKA STO FOURNO / BAKED FIGS WITH RED WINE

Figs are mostly eaten raw, sun dried or made into spoon sweets and jams. Fig trees are an intrinsic part of the Greek landscape. In the summer months, ripe figs are always plentiful.

12 ripe figs, washed	3 tablespoons red wine
2 teaspoons sugar	

Preheat the oven to 400°F. Score the top of each fig with a sharp knife. Place on a baking sheet. Sprinkle each fig with sugar and drizzle with the red wine. Bake for 12 to 15 minutes or until softened. Transfer to serving plates and spoon the thickened red wine sauce over the figs. Serve with yogurt or cream. [SERVES 4]

ABOVE: SUN-DRIED FIGS
RIGHT: SIKA STO FORNO /
BAKED FIGS WITH RED WINE

THE BASICS

IT IS EASY TO LEARN THE BASICS OF GREEK COOKING. MOST SAUCES SUCH AS THE CLASSIC *AVGOLEMONO* (EGG AND LEMON), *SKORDALIA* (GARLIC) OR *ASPRI SALTSA* (BÉCHAMEL) USED TO ENRICH MANY NATIONAL DISHES ARE UNCOMPLICATED. OTHER SAUCES TEND TO BE RICH REDUCTIONS OF STOCK, WINE, VINEGAR AND HERBS IN SLOW-SIMMERED MEAT AND VEGETABLE STEWS AND POT ROASTS. SUCH INGREDIENTS ARE ALSO COMBINED WITH MEAT JUICES IN THE FRYING PAN TO BE POURED OVER FINISHED MEAT DISHES.

The ancient Greeks were far more inventive. Apart from their use of *garum*-style fermented fish sauces made from anchovies, they also used a wide variety of herbs and spices—in particular silphium, caraway, aniseed, cumin and cheese—to enliven their sauces. Today, extra-virgin olive oil is always whisked with lemon juice, salt, black pepper and dried or fresh herbs to make *ladolemono*, which is drizzled over grilled or boiled fish. Together with *ladoxido* (olive oil and vinegar sauce), it can also be used as a sauce for simple salads and boiled vegetables such as *vlita* (amaranth) or *horta* (wild greens).

the bay leaves and allspice) and whisk constantly until the sauce thickens. Remove the saucepan from the heat and, when slightly cooled, stir in the cheese and nutmeg. [MAKES 4 CUPS]

SKORDALIA / GARLIC SAUCE

Although this popular sauce is often made with potatoes in restaurants, the best version is made with bread. In northern Greece, they also use walnuts as a thickener. It is always eaten with fried fish, especially galeos *(shark) and* bakaliaros *(salt cod) or vegetables, such as fried zucchini and eggplant or warm boiled beets or wild greens.*

3 slices bread, crusts removed	Dash freshly ground black
6 garlic cloves, peeled	pepper
1/2 teaspoon salt	4–5 tablespoons olive oil
2 tablespoons red wine vinegar	

Soak the bread in water for 10 to 15 minutes, then squeeze out all the excess moisture. Place the garlic cloves and salt in a mortar. Crush with the pestle until the garlic is puréed. Put the garlic, bread, vinegar and pepper into a food processor. Blend until smooth, slowly adding the oil while the blades are running. Cover and refrigerate until ready to use. [MAKES 1 CUP]

MEAT SAUCE

Meat sauce is used in many pastas, pies or stuffed vegetable dishes. I also use this aromatic sauce to make shepherd's pie or moussaka.

4 tablespoons olive oil	2 pounds lean ground beef
2 medium-sized yellow onions, peeled and diced	1/2 cup red wine
2 garlic cloves, finely chopped	1 fifteen-ounce can chopped tomatoes
2 celery stalks, peeled and diced	1 tablespoon tomato paste
3 tablespoons finely chopped fresh flat-leaf parsley	1 teaspoon cinnamon
1 teaspoon dried oregano	1 teaspoon allspice
1 sprig fresh thyme	2 bay leaves
	Salt
	Freshly ground black pepper

Heat 3 tablespoons of the olive oil in a large saucepan over medium heat, and sauté the onions, garlic, celery, parsley, oregano and thyme for about 5 minutes or until softened. Transfer this mixture to a bowl and reserve.

Add the remaining 1 tablespoon olive oil to the saucepan and sauté the ground beef, stirring constantly, for about 10 minutes or until the meat has browned. Add the red wine, tomatoes, tomato paste, cinnamon, allspice, bay leaves, salt and pepper and sauté for another 5 minutes. Return the onion, garlic and celery mixture to the saucepan, stir well and simmer the sauce for 45 to 60 minutes or until the sauce has thickened. [MAKES 5 CUPS]

TOMATO SAUCE

Add other ingredients such as fresh herbs or seafood to this basic sauce. Otherwise, simply drizzle it over grilled or baked fish and chicken.

5 tablespoons olive oil	2 pounds Roma tomatoes, peeled, seeded and finely chopped
1 garlic clove, peeled and finely diced	Salt
1 teaspoon dried oregano	Freshly ground black pepper

Heat the oil in a skillet over medium heat. Add the garlic and oregano and sauté for 5 minutes or until softened. Add the tomatoes and season to taste with salt and pepper. Simmer for 40 minutes, stirring occasionally. [MAKES 2 CUPS]

BÉCHAMEL SAUCE

Béchamel sauce is widely used in baked vegetable and meat dishes, such as the classic pastitsio *(baked pasta and meat pie). It also appears as a topping spread over zucchini or eggplant that have been stuffed with meat sauce.*

4 cups milk	1 cup all-purpose flour
2 bay leaves	3 tablespoons grated kefalotiri or parmesan cheese
1/2 teaspoon allspice berries	
8 tablespoons butter	1/2 teaspoon nutmeg

Heat the milk, bay leaves and allspice in a saucepan over low heat. Melt the butter in another saucepan, then add the flour and whisk for about 5 minutes until combined. Slowly ladle the hot milk into the flour mixture (discarding

LADOLEMONO SAUCE / OLIVE OIL AND LEMON DRESSING

This is the classic accompaniment to boiled fish, vegetables, prawns and lobster. It is also good as a salad dressing with boiled spinach or wild greens such as vlita *(amaranth).*

6 tablespoons olive oil	Salt
Juice of 1 lemon	Freshly ground black pepper

Mix the olive oil and lemon juice together in a bowl and season with salt and pepper to taste. Place in a serving bowl or in a jar in the refrigerator until ready to use. [**MAKES** ¹/₂ **CUP**]

PASTRY

Use this basic pastry recipe for all types of savory and fruit pies.

1 ²/₃ cups all-purpose flour	A pinch of salt
8 tablespoons cold butter, diced	1 egg
	3–5 tablespoons cold water

Put the flour, butter and salt into a food processor and blend until the mixture resembles breadcrumbs. Add the egg, then with the machine running, slowly add enough water to make a soft dough.

Form the dough into a disk, wrap in plastic film and refrigerate for at least 30 minutes before using according to the recipe instructions.

FILO (PHYLLO) PASTRY

Nowadays, commercial packages of filo are widely used in Greece. However, nothing surpasses homemade filo. It takes practice to achieve the paper-thin sheets made by accomplished Greek cooks. They use a special thin filo rolling pin (or broom handle) and a small round wooden table called a plasti, *which is set onto a flat surface for better manoeuvrability. This recipe is also suitable for all savory pies, although you would not use as many layers of dough as you would with commercial filo.*

3 ¹/₄ cups all-purpose flour	1 ¹/₂ cups water
1 teaspoon salt	6 tablespoons olive oil

Put the flour and salt into a large bowl. Make a well in the center and slowly add the water and olive oil, working the mixture by hand until it is smooth. Alternatively, blend the mixture in a food processor until smooth. Turn the dough onto a lightly floured surface. Knead until smooth and shiny, adding a little extra flour if necessary.

Form the dough into a disk, wrap in plastic wrap and refrigerate for at least 1 hour before using. Divide the dough into 8 balls. Roll each one out onto a large, lightly floured surface, carefully turning and stretching the filo sheet by hand into a thin 12-inch circle. Do not worry too much if some holes appear as these will be covered by the other filo layers used in any pie recipes. Leave the filo sheets to dry for 10 minutes before using.

KOURKOUTI / FRITTER BATTER

In Greek tavernas, battered and fried zucchini and eggplant are a very popular meze often served with skordalia. Other vegetables, such as cauliflower or asparagus, can also be used. Village cooks sometimes also add tomato juice and fresh or dried herbs to the batter. For a lighter batter that will produce a crisper coating, fold egg whites into the batter just before using.

1 cup all-purpose flour	1 cup water or beer
Salt	2 tablespoons olive oil
Pinch freshly ground black pepper	2 egg whites, stiffly beaten (optional)

Place the flour, salt and pepper in a bowl and mix well. Make a well in the middle and slowly add the water or beer and olive oil, whisking until blended. Cover the batter and rest for at least 30 minutes before using. If a lighter batter is desired, fold in the beaten egg whites just before using. [**MAKES 4 CUPS**]

THE GREEK STORE CUPBOARD

AVGOTARACHO

The dried and salted roe of *kefalos* (grey mullet) is highly prized in Greece. Many say that Greek *avgotaracho* is finer in flavor than its French and Italian counterparts, *poutargue* and *bottarga*. It is produced in the lagoons around Messolonghi where labyrinthine traps are used to catch the fish in the summer. Between August and September, the roes are salted intact for six hours, washed and then dried in the sun before being covered in beeswax. Thinly sliced with toast and a squeeze of lemon, intensely flavored avgotaracho makes a good accompaniment to ouzo. Before it became a luxury item, avgotaracho was commonly used as an ingredient when making *taramosalata*.

CAPERS / KAPARI

Kapari grow wild on most of the Greek islands. They are particularly prevalent in the Cyclades, where plants tumble over in-accessible cliffs and terraces or stifle old abandoned farmhouses and ruins. A staple of every household pantry, capers are picked in the summer months in the early evening when the flowers close and insects around the plants are less troublesome. The smallest buds and tiny cucumber-shaped fruits (*kaparagoura*) are the best for pickling or salting. On some islands, the larger fleshy buds are also picked just before they flower. They are boiled and served as a salad with olive oil and lemon.

CHEESE

Surprisingly perhaps, the Greeks are the largest consumers of *tiri* (cheese) in Europe. The majority of Greek cheeses are made from goat's and sheep's milk. Many islands also have indigenous varieties that never even make it to the cities of mainland Greece. Here are some of the most popular varieties:

ANTHOTIRO Lightly salted and creamy, this ricotta-like cheese is made from goat's milk and is used in sweet pastries and pies. It is also good for breakfast with honey and bread.

FETA The most famous Greek cheese is traditionally made from sheep's milk (or a combination of sheep's and goat's milk) and pickled in brine in wooden barrels. Some of the best feta comes from Dodoni in Epirus and Arahova in Parnassus. It ranges in flavor and texture from soft and creamy to hard and pungent.

GRAVIERA A Greek version of Swiss gruyère made from either sheep's or cow's milk. Yellow-colored, nutty and aromatic, some of the best graviera comes from Crete, Mytilini, Naxos and Tinos.

HALOUMI This popular Cypriot sheep's milk cheese is made by double-boiling the hot curds of cheese, which are then cut to allow salt and dried mint to be folded in between. With a texture similar to mozzarella, it is ideal grilled or pan-fried, then drizzled with olive oil and lemon juice.

KASSERI A mild, smooth-textured, pale yellow cheese made from sheep's or cow's milk. It is a good table cheese but it is most commonly used for *saganaki*, lightly dusted with flour then fried in olive oil and served with a squeeze of lemon.

KEFALOTIRI OR KEFALOGRAVIERA These two hard and tangy cheeses are made from goat's or sheep's milk. Hard grating cheeses, both are also good table cheeses, although kefalograviera is often also used for grilling or frying. Some of the best come from Crete, Naxos, Cephalonia and Epirus.

KOPANISTI Traditionally made in the Cyclades. The most famous comes from Mykonos, where it is left to ferment for several months in goat's skins until bacteria develop, giving kopanisti its characteristic pink colour and pungent flavor.

LADOTIRI Made in Mytilini and Zakinthos, this hard sheep's milk cheese is cured in olive oil and aged in wooden barrels for several months before being covered in a coating of wax.

MANOURI This creamy, soft sheep's milk cheese is frequently served with fruits and drizzled with honey.

MIZITHRA When fresh, this whey cheese is eaten as a soft table cheese, often used in pies and pastries. When aged, salted and hard, it is used as a grating cheese.

HERBS

BAY LEAF / DAFNI Widely used in soups and stews, marinades and spice mixes.

CORIANDER / KORIANDRON Although the leaves sometimes make their way into salads, it is the seeds that are mostly used to season sausages and pickles. In Cyprus, they are also one of the classic ingredients in *afelia*, a pork stew.

DILL / ANITHOS Used primarily in vegetable pies, meat and vegetable dishes such as *arni fricassee* (lamb and lettuce stew) and the classic Greek green salad comprising chopped romaine lettuce and green onions. Dried or fresh dill is also a component of *tzatziki* (cucumber and yogurt dip).

MINT / DIOSMOS Fresh mint is primarily added to pies and salads. Dried mint is also used sparingly in casseroles and stuffed vegetable dishes, and as an ingredient in meatballs, vegetable rissoles and *dolmades*.

OREGANO / RIGANI (*origanum vulgare*) and marjoram (*origanum marjorana*), which is closely related, grow wild all over Greece. After the long hot summers, the leaves and tight flower buds are dried. Every household posesses some *rigani*, ready to be sprinkled over grilled meat, fish or salads, or crumbled into rissoles, stews or sauces.

PARSLEY / MAIDANOS The most widely used herb in Greek cooking, it makes its way into sauces, stews and salads.

ROSEMARY / DENDROLIVANO Little used in cooking. The one exception is the dish *savoro*, in which rosemary and red wine vinegar are cooked with fish.

SAGE / FASKOMILO Dried sage leaves are made into a tea, often flavored with honey, that helps stomach complaints and colds.

SAVORY / THROUMBI Slightly stronger than oregano, dried savory is mostly added to grilled meat dishes.

THYME / THIMARI Although it also grows abundantly in the wild, thyme is rarely used, except as a substitute for oregano, sprinkled over grilled meat and fish.

HONEY / MELI

Greek thyme honey is still highly prized. Some of the best comes from islands in the Cyclades, such as Sikinos, Folegandros and

Anafi. Always used as a sweetener for pastries and desserts, it is also universally drizzled over yogurt or fresh fruits at the end of a meal.

LAKERDA / PRESERVED FISH

Fish, such as mackerel and bonito, that are salted, sliced and cured in olive oil are widely available in Greece. Together with salted sardines and anchovies, they are a popular meze or addition to salads.

NUTS AND DRIED FRUITS

PISTACHIOS / FISTIKIA are also used in pastries and desserts.

WALNUTS / KARIDIA and **ALMONDS / AMIGDALA** are used in many cakes, pastries and cookies. They also make their way into sauces for poultry and meat dishes. In northern Greece, *skordalia* (garlic sauce) is also made with walnuts as one of its main components.

DRIED GRAPES (golden raisins, currants and raisins) have always been an important export from Greece. Some of the best still come from the Ionian islands and Corinth. Dried grapes are used in both sweet and savory dishes, such as rice stuffings for vegetables and squid, or as a sweet-and-sour sauce for baked fish.

OLIVES / ELIES

Most rural families still preserve their own olives in salt or brine. They often also add lemon or orange peel, garlic, fennel, coriander seeds, rosemary, thyme or bay leaves to the cured olives, preserved in olive oil in jars or earthenware pots. Their color always depends on when they were picked and their state of ripeness. Green means they were picked at an early stage, purple to black at a later degree of ripeness.

TSAKISTES Cracked green olives are often used in cooking, especially in stews with squid or octopus, combined with fennel and other vegetables.

THROUMBES are black, wrinkled olives with a delicious prune-like flesh. Picked as late as possible, they are allowed to dry on the tree before being beaten off their branches onto tarpaulins spread on the ground. They are then salted and preserved.

The best known oval-shaped olives come from Kalamata in the Peloponnese. Other well-known varieties come from Volos and the Pelion region, Amfissa, Agriniou, Atalandi, Evia, Mytilini, Samos and Crete.

OLIVE OIL / ELAIOLADO

The third largest producer of olive oil in the world, Greece still sells much of its extra-virgin olive oil to Italy, where it is bottled and repackaged for export. In recent years, Greek producers are managing to export their own extra-virgin olive oil. Much of it is organic, widely available and generally cheaper than its Italian counterparts. Luckily, despite the changing diets of many young Greeks in the cities, olive oil consumption is still high in Greece. It notably contributes, along with the high intake of vegetables, pulses and fish in daily meals, to the wide-ranging health benefits of the "Mediterranean diet" that is alive and well in most of the country. If in Greece, look for *agourelaio*, the pungent new season's olive oil, which has a delicious fruity flavor and bright green color.

PASTOURMA

Hailing from Turkey and the Middle East, this highly spiced cured meat was originally made from camel. Today, it is made from beef. Sliced thinly, pastourma is eaten as a meze. Grated, it is often added to omelettes or pasta dishes.

PAXIMADIA / DRIED RUSKS

Every bakery sells different types of *paximadia*. Usually made from wheat or barley, they often include spices such as aniseed or coriander seed. They can be briefly softened in water and then added to soups or salads. Made into breadcrumbs, they can be used as a topping for stuffed vegetables and baked dishes, such as *pastitsio* and *moussaka*.

SPICES

ALLSPICE / BAHARI A common ingredient of béchamel sauce, allspice berries are also used in stews and meat sauces.

ANISEED / GLIKANISSO Widely used in ancient Greece, aniseed is mainly used today in biscuits and cakes, as a flavoring for ouzo and sausages, and in some fish dishes.

CINNAMON / KANELLA Cinnamon finds its way into sauces and stews, pastries and cookies. It is always sprinkled over *rizogalo* (rice pudding) and fried pastries such as *diples*.

CLOVES / GARIFALLA Whole cloves are added to stews and sauces; ground cloves are added to breads, cookies and sweets.

CUMIN / KIMINO Cumin is added to *soutzoukakia* and *stifado*.

FENNEL / MARATHOS These seeds are added to sausage mixes, pickles, breads and some fish and pork stews.

MAHLEP MAHLEPI These dried seeds of a wild cherry tree are often used in Turkish and Middle Eastern cooking. In Greece, they are boiled, then pounded, and are used as a flavoring for festive breads and some cakes.

MASTIC MASTICHA The resinous sap collected from the *pistacia lentiscus* tree that grows on the island of Chios is used to flavor sweets, breads, ice creams, the sugar fondant *vanillia* and a liqueur called *masticha*. Popular with the sultans of the Ottoman Empire, who chewed it and gave it to their harems as a natural breath freshener, it is still used as chewing gum today in Greece.

NUTMEG / MOSCHOKARIDO Like allspice, it is used in béchamel, stews, sauces and some sweets.

SESAME SEEDS / SOUSSAMI The seeds are mostly sprinkled over breads, pies, cookies and *pastelli*, a sesame sweet offered at weddings. *Tahini*, sesame paste, is used to make *hummus* and the Lenten fasting soup *tahinosoupa*.

SAFFRON / KROKOS Although highly prized by the ancient Greeks, both as a food spice and a dye for coloring cloth, saffron is not widely used today. Although, it is grown in Kozani in northern Greece, most of it is for export. Some is used locally to color and flavor homemade spirits. It is also required for some cookies and cake recipes.

VINEGAR / XIDI

Wine vinegars have been an indispensible part of the Greek kitchen since ancient times. Many meat and game stews, such as *stifado*, use vinegar as an important flavoring.

WINES AND SPIRITS

In the past decade, Greek wines have finally begun to gain recognition. Small boutique wineries are producing world-class wines using modern wine-making methods on some of the country's interesting indigenous grape varieties. With over 300 unique and unusual grapes to choose from, the results have been impressive. Even *retsina*, that famous wine that most visitors cannot stomach, has (sadly for some people) begun to have less pine resin added to it.

OUZO Traditionally distilled from grapes, ouzo is a clear spirit flavored with a variety of herbs and spices such as aniseed, star anise, coriander, cloves, citrus peel, caraway, mastic and fennel. It is best drunk at room temperature, served with ice or water.

TSIPOURO from central and northern mainland Greece, and **RAKI** from Crete, are both the Greek equivalent of grappa, fiery distillates made by families after the grape harvest. They are best served with food.

YOGURT / YAOURTI

Thick Greek yogurt is used for marinades, sauces, cakes, pies and savory dishes. It is also a common and cleansing dessert, simply served with walnuts and drizzled with honey.

BIBLIOGRAPHY

Athenaeus, *The Deipnosophists*. The Loeb Classical Library 7 volumes. London: William Heinemann, 1969.

Barron, Rosemary. *Flavours of Greece*. London: Penguin Books, 1991.

Baumann, Hellmut. *Greek Wild Flowers and Plant Lore in Ancient Greece*. London: The Herbert Press, 1993.

Chantiles, Vilma Liacouras. *The Food of Greece*. New York: Atheneum, 1975.

Davidson, Alan. *Mediterranean Seafood*. London: Penguin Books, 1972.

Eden, Esen and Stavroulakis, Nicholas. *Salonika A Family Cookbook*. Athens: Talos Press, 1997.

Gray, Patience. *Honey from a Weed*. London: Prospect Books, 1986.

Harris, Andy. *A Taste of the Aegean, Greek Cooking and Culture*. London: Pavilion Books, 1992.

Howe, Robin. *The Mediterranean Diet*. London: Wiedenfeld & Nicholson, 1985.

Kochilas, Diane. *The Food and Wine of Greece*. New York: St. Martin's Press, 1990.

Kremezi, Aglaia. *The Foods of Greece*. New York: Stewart, Tabori & Chang, 1993.

Lambert-Gocs, Miles. *The Wines of Greece*. London: Faber and Faber, 1990.

Louis, Diana Farr and Marinos, June. *Prospero's Kitchen: Mediterranean Cooking of the Ionian Islands*. New York: M.Evans and Company, 1995.

Mabey, Richard. *Plants with a Purpose*. London: Collins, 1977.

Manessis, Nico. *The Greek Wine Guide*. Corfu: Olive Press, 1996.

Mark, Theonie. *Greek Islands Cooking*. London: Batsford, 1978.

Phillips, Roger. *Wild Food*. London: Pan Books, 1983.

Sfikas, George. *Medicinal Plants of Greece*. Athens: Efstathiadis Group, 1985.

Stavroulakis, Nicholas. *Cookbook of the Jews of Greece*. Athens: Lycabettus Press, 1986.

Stubbs, Joyce M. *The Home Book of Greek Cookery*. London: Faber and Faber, 1967.

Tselemendes, Nicolas. *Greek Cooking*. New York: DC Divry, 1956.

Wolfert, Paula. *Mostly Mediterranean*. New York: Penguin Books, 1996.

Wolfert, Paula. *Mediterranean Grains and Greens*. New York: Harper Collins, 1998.

Yannoulis, Anne. *Greek Calendar Cookbook*. Athens: Lycabettus Press, 1988.

ACKNOWLEDGMENTS

There are many people who helped with this book, both in practical and more subtle ways. I would like to thank all of them, and also anyone that I may have inadvertently forgotten:

My photographer William Meppem, who achieved the impossible in just two weeks of frantic shooting; Con Nemitsas and James Demetriou of Demcos for the seafood; Anthony Puharich of Vic's Meat for all the meat, poultry and game; Justyn McGrigor of Murdoch Produce and Matt Brown of Matt Brown's Greens for the fruit and vegetables; Ray and June Henman of The Salad Farm for assorted herbs and salad leaves; Simon Johnson for indispensable foodstuffs such as olive oil and vinegar; Peter Brescanini of Estate Wines for the Greek wines; George Vasili of Global Foods for cheeses and olives; Christos Carras of Stater Ltd. for Greek artisan food products; Sibella Court for kindly lending us her prop collection; the potter Malcolm Greenwood for making us some beautiful dishes and bowls; Rebecca Black for her tireless assistance in the studio kitchen; Philip Noel-Baker for allowing me to write and cook at Candili in Evia; Trevor Hopkins for sanctuary in London; Tim Olsen, Dominique Ogilvie and Elizabeth King for their appreciative recipe tasting at odd hours; Jane Mackay for stolen days out of the office; Sharyn Storrier Lyneham for bringing me to Australia; Joan Campbell for words of wisdom in her daily telephone calls; Aphrodite Georgiadou for Greek spelling corrections and so much more; Aphrodite's mother, the late Jenny Georgiadou, who taught me many recipes in her kitchen; Nicos Caracostas for showing me remote islands in the Aegean; Nicos Mangriotis for accompanying me in my incessant quest for the best tavernas in Athens; Costas Tsingas for the late-night culinary conversations; Emma Ross for designing the book; my publisher Pam Brewster and everyone at Hodder Headline Australia for their patience when I suddenly started a new life and job in America; and finally to all the Greek cooks and chefs, fishermen and farmers, market stall-holders and food artisans who have shared their secrets of the land and sea with me.

TABLE OF EQUIVALENTS

The exact equivalents in the following tables have been rounded for convenience.

LIQUID/DRY MEASURES

U.S.	Metric
1/4 teaspoon	1.25 milliliters
1/2 teaspoon	2.5 milliliters
1 teaspoon	5 milliliters
1 tablespoon (3 teaspoons)	15 milliliters
1 fluid ounce (2 tablespoons)	30 milliliters
1/4 cup	60 milliliters
1/3 cup	80 milliliters
1/2 cup	120 milliliters
1 cup	240 milliliters
1 pint (2 cups)	480 milliliters
1 quart (4 cups, 32 ounces)	960 milliliters
1 gallon (4 quarts)	3.84 liters
1 ounce (by weight)	28 grams
1 pound	454 grams
2.2 pounds	1 kilogram

OVEN TEMPERATURE

Fahrenheit	Celsius	Gas
250	120	1/2
275	140	1
300	150	2
325	160	3
350	180	4
375	190	5
400	200	6
425	220	7
450	230	8
475	240	9
500	260	10

INDEX

A

amaranth salad, 44, 45
anchovies
  double-fried and stuffed, 110
  fried, 34, 35
  marinated with potato and onion
    salad, 24, 25
anginares
  a la polita, 55
  me araka, 55
arakas yiachni, 52
arni
  "fricassee", 94, 96
  me anginares, 92
  sto harti, 95, 96
artichokes
  and lamb stew, 92
  Constantinople style, 55
  marinated raw, 28, 29
  stewed, 55
avgolemono, 39

B

bakaliaros
  me prassorizo, 110, 111
  me skordalia, 114
baked
  beef with orzo, 102
  figs with red wine, 148, 149
  lima beans, 26, 28
  lobster with tomatoes, 116, 117
  prawns with tomatoes and
    feta, 118, 119
baklavas, 142
barbounia sto fourno me ambelofila,
  123
béchamel sauce, 152
beef
  baked with orzo, 102
  smyrna-style rissoles, 105
beets, shallot, dandelion and chicken
  liver salad, 44
black-eyed pea
  and chard stew, 65
  salad, 62, 63
boiled snapper and bream with
    vegetables, 112, 113
bonito
  and samphire salad, 34, 35
  grilled with fennel, 117
bourdetto, 123, 125
bourekakia, 36, 37
braised
  leeks and tomatoes, 28, 29
  veal with garlic, parsley and
    vinegar, 98
brandada me domates, 126
brandade with tomatoes and
  onions, 126
briam, 52
bulgur wheat salad, 62, 63

C

Cephalonian meat pie, 72, 74
cheese
  feta and mint dip, 12
  feta and pepper dip, 20, 21

feta and red bell pepper, 21, 23
  fried, 21, 22
  halloumi, banana chiles, cherry
    tomato and escarole salad, 48, 49
  pastries, 68, 70
  sweet, 138, 139
chicken
  baked in yogurt with spinach, 80, 82,
    83
  fritters, 32
  livers, 44
  pie, 72, 73
  roast, with stuffing, orzo and garlic,
    84, 85
  spicy, with fried potatoes, 86, 88
  stew, 82
  with zucchini, green olives and green
    garlic, 82
chickpea
  and orzo soup, 58
  fritters, 30, 31
chiles
  banana, 28, 29
Christmas shortcake, 137, 138
cod
  roe dip, 10
  with leek rice, 110, 111
  with skordalia, 114
crab fritters, 32, 34
cucumber, garlic and yogurt dip, 12
custard pies, 142, 143
cuttlefish and spinach stew, 119, 121

D

deep-fried pastries dipped in honey,
  144, 147
diples, 144, 147
dips
  cod roe, 10
  cucumber, garlic and yogurt, 12
  eggplant, 12
  feta and mint dip, 12
  lima bean dip, 10
  parsley, 12
  spicy feta and pepper dip, 20, 21
domates gemistes, 38, 40
domatokeftedes, 30, 31
domatorizo, 58
dolmades, 14, 17
dried bread rusks
  with artichokes and feta, 18
  with tomatoes and capers, 18

E

eggplant
  and veal stew, 98, 101
  baked with tomato and cheese, 52
  baked with zucchini and potatoes, 52
  dip, 12
  fried, 10
  papoutsakia, 52, 53
eggs
  scrambled with tomatoes, 18, 19
eliopsomo, 76, 77

F

fakes salata, 62, 63

faki, 60
faskomilo, 134, 136
fassoulada, 64, 65
fava, 10, 11
fennel pastries, fried, 68, 70
feta
  and mint dip, 12
  and pepper dip, 20, 21
  and red bell pepper, 21, 23
  horiatiki, 39, 40, 42
  zucchini and mint salad, 43, 44
figs, baked with red wine, 148, 149
filo pastry, 153
fish and shellfish
  anchovies
    double-fried and stuffed, 110
    fried 34, 35
    marinated with potato and onion
      salad, 24, 25
  bonito
    grilled with fennel, 117
    pickled, and samphire salad, 34, 35
  cod
    brandade with tomatoes and
      onions, 126
    with leek rice, 110, 111
    with skordalia, 114
  cuttlefish and spinach stew, 119, 121
  fritters, 32
  kingfish with skordalia, 122, 123
  leatherjackets, "savoro" style, 119,
    120
  lobster with tomatoes, 116, 117
  mackerel, baked "plaki" style, 110
  mussels
    stuffed, 34, 35
    with red wine sauce, 118, 119
  octopus
    pickled with garlic, parsley and
      olive oil, 24
    stewed with red wine and onions,
      125
  prawns with tomatoes and feta, 118,
    119
  red mullet baked in vine leaves, 123
  sardines
    baked, with green pepper, 110
    marinated with onion salad, 117
  scallops, pan-fried 34, 35
  seafood, feta and red pepper pies,
    75, 76
  snapper and bream with vegetables,
    112, 113
  squid
    stuffed, 126, 127
    with onions and lemon juice, 114
  soup, 113
  spicy stew, 123, 125
  swordfish
    marinated with tomatoes, 125
    spiced fillets with amaranth, 124,
      125
  tuna stew, 113
  whitebait "marinato", 114
  whiting, stuffed in vine leaves with
    bulgar wheat, 26

fried
  banana chiles, 28, 29
  eggplants and zucchini with
    skordalia, 10
fritters
  batter, 153
  chicken, 32
  chickpea, 30, 31
  crab, 32, 34
  fish, 32
  tomato, 30, 31
  wild greens, 32
  zucchini, 30, 31

G

galaktoboureko, 142, 143
garides saganaki, 118, 119
garlic sauce, 152
gavros
  diplotigania, 110
  tiganitos, 34, 35
gigantes plaki, 26, 28
grape must dessert, 130, 131
Greek
  bean soup, 64, 65
  coffee, 130, 132
  Easter bread, 78, 79
  guinea fowl "krassato", 84

H

halloumi, banana chiles, cherry tomato
  and escarole salad, 48, 49
halvas, 141, 142
hirino
  gemisto, 106, 107
  me prassa, 105
  selino avgolemono, 102
honey balls, 148
honeyed biscuits, 134, 137
horiatiki, 39, 40, 42
hortokeftedes, 32
hortopita, 78

I

ipovrihio, 134

J

jellied ham, 106

K

kalamarikia gemista, 126, 127
katsikaki or arni sto fourno, 90, 92
kavourokeftedes, 32, 34
kebabs, 37
  lamb, 36, 37
  pork and coriander, 36, 37
kefalonitiki kreatopita, 72, 74
keftedes, 31, 32, 37
  domatokeftedes, 30, 31
  hortokeftedes, 32
  kavourokeftedes, 32, 34
  kotokeftedes, 32
  kolokithokeftedes, 30, 31
  psarokeftedes, 32
  revithokeftedes, 30, 31
kid roast, 90, 92
kingfish with skordalia, 122, 123

kohlrabi, 46
kolios plaki, 110
kolitsani, 9
kolokithokeftedes, 30, 31
kolokithokorfades, 14, 15
kolokithopita, 78
kotokeftedes, 32
kotopita, 72, 73
kotopoulo
  kapama, 86, 88
  psito me gemista ke kritharaki,
    84, 85
kouneli stifado, 102, 103
kourabiedes, 137, 138
kourkouti, 153
kritamo, 26
ktenia, 34, 35

L
ladolemono sauce, 153
ladera, 39
lamb
  and artichoke stew, 92
  and lettuce stew, 94, 96
  baked in parchment paper, 95, 96
  filets with zucchini, potato and
    capers, 96, 97
  kebabs, 36, 37
  "kleftiko", 106
  legato, 92, 93
  loin, stuffed, 92
  meatballs, 36, 37
  rack, stuffed with feta and mint, 96
  roast, 90, 92
  tomato, garlic and lemon stew, 92, 93
leatherjackets, "savoro" style, 119, 120
leeks and tomatoes, 28, 29
lentil
  and leek soup, 63
  salad, 62, 63
  soup, 60
lima beans
  baked, 26, 28
  dip, 10
liver, marinated, 36, 37
lobster with tomatoes, 116, 117
loukoumades, 148

M
mackerel, baked "plaki" style, 110
maidanosalata, 12
marinated
  anchovy, potato and onion salad, 24,
    25
  liver, 36, 37
  mushrooms, 28, 29
  raw artichokes, 28, 29
  sardines, 117
mavromatika
  me seskoula, 65
  piaz, 62, 63
meat
  and pasta pie, 66, 67
  pastries, 36, 37
  sauce, 153
melitinia, 138, 139
melitzanes sto fourno, 52
melitzanosalata, 12
melomakarona, 134, 137
midia
  gemista, 34, 35
  krassata, 118, 119
moschari
  giouvetsi me kritharaki, 102
  me melitzanes, 98, 101
moussaka, 54, 55
moustalevria, 130, 131
mushrooms, 28, 29
mussels
  stuffed, 34, 35

with red wine sauce, 118, 119
myatico me skordalia, 122, 123

O
octapodi
  krassato, 125
  skordato, 24
octopus
  pickled with garlic, parsley and olive
    oil, 24
  stewed with red wine and onions, 125
olive bread, 76, 77
olive oil and lemon dressing, 153
orange and pomegranate jelly, 148
ortika se klimatofila me pligouri, 88, 89

P
pan-fried
  scallops, 34, 35
  squid with onions and lemon juice,
    114
papoutsakia, 52, 53
parsley dip, 12
partridge "salmi" with rice, 87, 88
pasta
  meat and pasta pie, 66, 67
  spinach, parsley and yogurt, 66
pastitsio, 66, 67
pastry, 153
  filo, 153
  whorls, 144, 147
peas
  artichokes and, 55
  stewed, 52
phakos ke prasson, 63
pickled
  octopus with garlic, parsley and
    olive oil, 24
  tassel hyacinth bulbs, 26, 27
pies and pastries
  baklavas, 142
  Cephalonian meat pie, 72, 74
  cheese pastries, 68, 70
  chicken pie, 72, 73
  custard pies, 142, 143
  deep-fried pastries, 144, 147
  fennel pastries, 68, 70
  meat and pasta pie, 66, 67
  meat pastries, 36, 37
  pastry, 153
  pastry whorls, 144, 147
  seafood, feta and red pepper pies,
    75, 76
  spanakopita, 70, 71
  spinach pies, 29
  sweet cheese pastries, 138, 139
  wild greens pie, 78
pikti, 106
pligouri salata, 62, 63
potato, onion and caper salad, 46, 47
pork
  and coriander kebabs, 36, 37
  and leek stew, 105
  loin, stuffed, 106, 107
  with celery, 102
pot-roasted veal with pasta, 98, 100
prassa me domates, 28, 29
prawns, baked with tomatoes and feta,
  118, 119
psarokeftedes, 32
purslane, smoked trout, potato and
  quail egg salad, 40, 41

Q
quail in vine leaves, 88, 89

R
rabbit stew, 102, 103
red mullet baked in vine leaves, 123
revani, 138, 140

revithokeftedes, 30, 31
rice pudding, 146, 147
rissoles, smyrna-style, 105
rizogalo, 146, 147
roast
  chicken with stuffing, orzo and garlic,
    84, 85
  kid or lamb with lemon potatoes, 90,
    92
  quail in vine leaves with bulgur wheat
    pilaf, 88, 89
roasted feta and red bell pepper, 21, 23

S
saganaki, 21, 22
sage tea, 134, 136
salads, 39
  black-eyed pea, 62, 63
  boiled amaranth, 44, 45
  boiled zucchini, feta and mint, 43, 44
  bulgur wheat, 62, 63
  golden beet, shallot, dandelion and
    chicken liver, 44
  halloumi, banana chiles, cherry
    tomato and escarole, 48, 49
  horiatiki, 40, 42
  marinated anchovy, potato and onion,
    24, 25
  marinated raw artichokes, 28, 29
  pickled bonito and samphire, 34, 35
  potato, onion and caper, 46, 47
  purslane, smoked trout, potato and
    quail egg, 40, 41
samphire, pickled, 26
sardelles
  marinates me kremmidia, 117
  sto fourno, 110
sardines
  baked with green pepper, 110
  marinated with onion salad, 117
sauces
  béchamel, 152
  garlic, 152
  ladolemono, 153
  meat, 152
  olive oil and lemon dressing, 153
  skordalia, 152
  tomato, 152
sausage and pepper stew, 104, 105
scallops, pan-fried, 34, 35
scrambled eggs and tomatoes, 18, 19
seafood, feta and red pepper pies, 75,
  76
semolina
  and almond cake, 138, 140
  pudding, 141, 142
sika sto fourno, 148, 149
skaltsounia, 68, 70
skordalia, 152
smyrna-style rissoles, 105
snapper and bream with vegetables,
  112, 113
sofrito, 98, 99
soupies me spanaki, 119, 121
soups
  chickpea and orzo, 58
  fish, 113
  Greek bean, 64, 65
  lentil, 60
    and leek, 63
  tahinosoupa, 56, 60
  trachanas and tomato, 58, 59
sour-cherry preserve, 134, 135
soutzoukakia smirneika, 105
spanakopita, 70, 71
spanakopites, 29
spanakorizo, 58
spetsofai, 104, 105
spicy
  chicken with fried potatoes, 86, 88

feta and pepper dip, 20, 21
spinach
  pies, 29
  rice, 58
squid
  stuffed, 126, 127
  with onions and lemon juice, 114
strapatsada, 18, 19
stridia, 9
stuffed
  kohlrabi, 46
  lamb loin, 92
  mussels, 34, 35
  pork loin, 106, 107
  rack of lamb, 96
  squid, 126, 127
  tomatoes, 38, 40
  vine leaves, 14, 17
  zucchini flowers, 14
submarine, 134
sweet cheese pastries, 138, 139
swordfish
  marinated with tomatoes, 125
  spiced fillets with amaranth, 124, 125

T
tahinosoupa, 56, 60
taramosalata, 10
tassel hyacinth, 26, 27
tomato
  fritters, 30, 31
  rice, 58
  sauce, 152
  stuffed three different ways, 38, 40
tonos stifado, 113
trachanas and tomato soup, 58, 59
trachanosoupa, 58, 59
tsoureki, 78, 79
tuna stew, 113
tzatziki, 12

V
veal
  and eggplant stew, 98, 101
  and rice balls, 60, 61
  braised with garlic, parsley and
    vinegar, 98
  pot-roasted with pasta, 98, 100
vegetables à la grecque, 46
vine leaves
  stuffed, 14, 17
  stuffed with bulgar wheat and
    whiting, 26
vissino gliko, 134, 135
volvi, 26, 27

W
whitebait "marinato", 114
wild greens
  fritters, 32
  pie, 78

X
xerotigana, 144, 147
xiphias
  marinatos, 125
  me vlita, 124, 125

Y
yellow split pea purée with onions and
  capers, 10
youvarlakia, 60, 61

Z
zucchini
  feta and mint salad, 43, 44
  flowers, 14
    omelette, 14, 16
    stuffed, 14, 15
  fritters, 30, 31
  moussaka, 54, 55